TOPICS IN AUTISM

Seeing Is Believing

VIDEO SELF-MODELING FOR PEOPLE WITH AUTISM
AND OTHER DEVELOPMENTAL DISABILITIES

Tom Buggey, Ph.D.

Sandra L. Harris, Ph.D., series editor

Woodbine House ◆ 2009

Photo credits: pages 6, 115, and cover, courtesy of Deborah Luehrs; pages 32, 52, and 107, courtesy of Kathleen Greeson; pages 39, 40, 67, and 84 courtesy of Tom Buggey

Library of Congress Cataloging-in-Publication Data

Buggey, Tom.
  Seeing is believing : video self-modeling for people with autism and other develop-mental disabilities / Tom Buggey. -- 1st ed.
      p. cm.
  Includes bibliographical references and index.
  ISBN 978-1-890627-88-1 (pbk.)
  1. Autistic children--Education--Audio-visual aids.. 2. Developmentally disabled children--Education--Audio-visual aids. I. Title.

 LC4717.B84 2009
 371.94--dc22
                                                                                        2008052057

Manufactured in the United States of America

First Edition

10   9   8   7   6   5   4   3   2   1

To my family:
John and Betty for shaping my early life, thus my entire life,
Ann, for being the perfect partner,
Andrea and Jennifer,
and to one of my boyhood role models,
Roberto Clemente, who noticed a shy boy at the back of a
crowd of autograph hounds.

Table of Contents

Introduction

Students with autism present parents and educators with a great challenge. How do you educate children who have difficulty attending to a task, and who sometimes set up a range of defenses designed specifically to avoid attending to the people instructing them?

To date, the instructional approach with the best track record with children with autism is intense application of Applied Behavior Analysis (ABA) (Lovaas, 1987). This method requires forty hours of home- or clinic-based instruction per week and is ideally begun before the child reaches the age of three and a half. The approach was originally criticized for the use of aversives (punishment); however, changes in the procedures over the years have resulted in a much more positive and engaging approach. ABA as it is currently practiced typically employs an array of naturalistic teaching methods, and, especially with young children, attempts to follow the child's lead during playful interactions.

Although ABA is an effective instructional approach, it is very important that we continue to explore and evaluate new methods of teaching children and adults on the autism spectrum that may enhance ABA methods or provide alternatives.

For the past 14 years, the author and others have been researching a method in which children serve as their own instructional models: video self-modeling (VSM). Video self-modeling can be defined as the manipulation of videos so that a person is able to watch himself performing a behavior correctly or at an advanced level. For example, a child might be filmed saying individual words. These words can be clipped and saved using the video editing software that comes free with all PCs and Macs. Using this same software, the user can easily drag and drop the recorded words to form sentences that are slightly more advanced than the child is presently able to put together. Similarly, a child who tends to display aggressive behaviors in certain situations can be videotaped during role playing activities in which he acts appropriately in these situations. The person thus serves as both the model and the viewer. I want to emphasize the positive nature of self-modeling. Videos are edited so that only the best examples of a behavior are viewed.

Because of the research underlying the use of video modeling (typically involving peers or adults as models), this technique has become very attractive to behavior analysts looking for engaging ways to teach essential skills to people on the autism spectrum. By allowing children to act as their own models, we may be able to considerably strengthen the effects that video modeling has on the viewer. The research base for VSM as a treatment for children with autism and other developmental disorders has been growing, and the evidence indicates that in many cases it can have a strong impact. However, the method is not widely used, possibly due to ignorance or fear of the technology.

The purpose of this book is to present the case for video self-modeling and to provide a how-to manual for anyone who would like to try it. The book is designed to be a guide for teachers, counselors, therapists, and, most importantly, parents. Video self-modeling has been shown to be effective for children and students, aged two and up, of any ability level. As long as someone can attend to a video and recognize himself, he should be able to benefit from VSM.

The Author and His Work

In 1992, I was a doctoral student at Penn State University looking for a topic for my dissertation. My goal was to find an area of study where I would have the greatest impact possible on children with disabilities, so I had enrolled in the Early Intervention program and begun studies of language development and interventions. Being able to intervene at the earliest age possible, and on a skill highly related to later academic and social success, seemed to meet my requirements. I also wanted my dissertation to be one of maximum impact.

I soon found that many studies noted a problem regarding language intervention: behaviors seen in the clinic or during intervention failed to generalize or transfer to settings other than the one in which they were taught. That is, the children would gladly perform for the therapists, but often would not use their new skills in their regular everyday interactions. This so-called *generalization* of skills is an essential outcome of instruction. It means that a child will repeat a skill in different circumstances than those in which he originally learned to use the skill. For example, a student who has learned to make change in a math lesson will be able to use the skill at the store, or a child who learns new words in the preschool therapy room will be able to use them on the playground. After learning about these problems with generalization, I searched the research literature for methods that had strong evidence of a generalization effect to see if any might be useful for language instruction.

One day, the chair of my dissertation committee, John Neisworth, handed me an article about teaching parenting skills written by S. S. Meharg and L. E. Lipsker (1991). (I was fortunate to have an exceptional dissertation committee at Penn State that also included Charles Hughes, Janice Light, and John Salvia.) I thought the article was a bit unrelated, but as I read through it I could see possible applications. The researchers had filmed parents interacting with their children in play settings. They then edited the tape so that only the most positive interactions were illustrated and allowed the parents to view the movies. Subsequently, the parents significantly increased their rate of positive interactions, and, more importantly for my research, the behavior **generalized** from the therapy setting to the home.

It was not a stretch to see how this video technique could be applied to language therapy/intervention. In the Head Start program where I would carry out my research, the children were already imitating advanced language use with the therapist and teacher. All I had to do was capture the imitations and allow the children to view themselves talking at an advanced level. The children would then serve as their own models. Easy. This is how I started on the road to video self-modeling as a research agenda.

I can say that what I did was far from easy—except for the technology part. By choosing language as my target, I sentenced myself (pun intended) to countless hours of transcribing and listening to audiotapes over and over again to hear whether the students (who were between three and a half and four years old) were using the particular language form I had targeted. The behavior I chose was the contractible copula form of the verb "to be" (any use of the verb that can be contracted, such as saying "He my friend" instead of "He's my friend" or "I going" instead of "I'm going").

We filmed the children imitating sentences using the correct form in a teacher area that was apart from the classroom space and free from most distractions. I then learned how to edit VHS tapes by hooking up the camera to a VCR. The resulting videos were very crude with breaks between each sentence. (I didn't realize then that pushing "pause" rather than "stop" would eliminate these snow-filled breaks in the video.) Even so, the children were able to view themselves correctly using the "to be" verb in sentences, and they were elated to see themselves on TV—even in this crude form.

To ensure that the children were generalizing their use of contractions, we placed micro-tape recorders in fanny packs around their waists and attached lapel microphones to their shirts when they went outside for playtime and prior to lunch. I listened to three hours of tape a night, while a graduate assistant listened to about a third that much to make sure what I was hearing was accurate. The children all dramatically increased their use of "to be" and its contractions in their typical play environments.

(Let me interject here that I feel one of the reasons self-modeling is not more widely used is that the technology intimidates people. Editing videos seems like something better suited to a Hollywood studio than the average person's living room. I will get into the how-to later in the book, but let me say this; the proverbial "If I can do it, you can do it" line never had a more appropriate application. I panic when the number of cables or buttons exceeds two, but have found the editing process to be both easy and fun when using either a camcorder-VCR connection or a computer with video-editing software.)

I have now been investigating the potentials of video self-modeling for 15 years. Some of my work is published, but most of it has involved working with individuals in situations that lacked the rigor to be written up in professional journals. Over the years, I have continued to look at language development, but have tended to be drawn into situations involving children with autism, behavior disorders, and attention deficit disorders. The majority of the requests I have received have been for shaping children's social behaviors along with a few requests for improving functional and language skills.

Self-modeling was not successful every time I used it; however, it was effective a large majority of the time. One of the attributes of self-modeling is that positive results are seen almost immediately. If gains are not seen after the individual has viewed the video a few times, you know to move on to another method or to go back and reassess the video content. The positive results we have seen with VSM have varied from moderate gains to almost immediate mastery of a skill or total elimination of a behavior. Details of some of these cases will appear later in this book.

Using Video Self-Modeling with Students with Autism

The first controlled study I conducted with students with autism occurred in 1997 (Buggey, Toombs, Gardner, & Cerveti, 1998). My graduate students and I worked with three middle school students with moderate to severe autism as we tried to teach them to respond verbally to questions. The students could not or would not imitate, so we had to ask questions repeatedly over time and tape for long periods to gather enough responses to create a two- to three-minute video. One of the students only responded twice so we looped these responses onto a one-and-a-half-minute tape.

The students made nice gains after viewing their tapes, and their parents commented on the increase in responsiveness. When we looked at the data more closely, we found an interesting pattern concerning specific questions. We had let the questions flow naturally in the play environment and incorporated common questions into a list of ones already scripted. We found that the students responded 100 percent of the time to some questions, but did not respond at all to others. Questions beginning with "how" and "why" were very problematic, while questions asking for names of people, things, or colors were more easily mastered. If we had been more selective with the types of question we used, the results probably would have been even more dramatic. I was intrigued by the results, but my main interest remained in preschool language development.

A turning point in my research came during a trip to Louisville in 1998. I was invited by the Kentucky Department of Education to present at a teacher workshop on the use of self-modeling to modify behavior. My host for the event was Preston Lewis, a behavior consultant for the state. After my presentation, he approached me and asked if I had read Temple Grandin's new book, *Thinking in Pictures* (1996). (Temple Grandin has written several books on her life with autism and is presently an associate professor at Colorado State University.) Soon afterwards, I bought a copy of the book and eagerly started reading. I remember little of the book, not because it wasn't very good, but because the impact of the first paragraph overshadowed all else. I quote the first part of it here:

> *"I THINK IN PICTURES. Words are like a second language to me. I translate both spoken and written words into full-color movies, complete with sound, which run like a VCR tape in my head. When somebody speaks to me, his words are instantly translated into pictures" (p.1).*

It was the VCR analogy that resulted in a mini-epiphany for me. I knew that everybody with autism did not think like Grandin; however, many probably did. I was always intrigued by how children with autism built up so many defense mechanisms to guard against social interactions with flesh and blood humans, including parents and teachers, yet they could sit for hours and watch two-dimensional humans without a hint of discomfort or distress. Grandin's book became the inspiration for the research I have conducted over the past ten years, which, for the most part, has focused on children with autism.

As a professor at the University of Memphis, I did some research in self-modeling, but I had immersed myself so deeply into community service programs and grants that it was difficult to find the necessary time. Then in January of 2007, I was honored to be appointed as the Siskin Children's Institute Chair of Excellence in Early Childhood Special Education at the University of Tennessee-Chattanooga. This was an endowed position in collaboration with the Siskin Children's Institute, an organization serving preschoolers with disabilities in an inclusive environment. It was the association with Siskin that precipitated the move. I would be in a wonderful environment where the expectation was *research.*

The Siskin Children's Institute now houses the Center for Self-Modeling Studies, where we focus our efforts on using self-modeling with children with pervasive developmental delay and autistic-like symptoms as well as other students with developmental delays. Working in a preschool allows us to more closely examine details of self-modeling, some of which have never been addressed. For example, at what ages does self-modeling become effective? Is it directly related to self-recognition? Are there attention thresholds that can be identified that could serve as minimal requirements for self-modeling use? In addition we are inviting parents and educators to become partners in our research efforts.

The Siskin Children's Institute also serves as the home for the companion website for this book and offers resources and technical assistance for individuals who are using self-modeling. A unique element to this website is that it is designed to serve as a clearinghouse for stories, anecdotes, criticisms, and research results related to self-modeling. Parents who try the method with their children are encouraged to write for suggestions, relate what worked and what didn't, and submit the results of their efforts. The site can be found on the web at www.siskinvsm.org.

Research on self-modeling is still in its infancy, although work in this area began in the early 1970s. Development has been slow. The number of studies is still relatively small and the number of researchers focusing on children with autism is low, with only a handful of studies being published. (In their meta-analyses study in 2007, S. Bellini, J. Akullian, and A. Hopf found eight such studies. There are also two studies of mine that came out shortly after Bellini's article.) Yet, the results found so far, especially with children with milder forms of autism, have been so dramatic that I think this trend will change. It is my hope that in some small way this book will be a catalyst for this change.

1 | The Science Behind Self-Modeling

Background

Modeling is a key element in every child's education. This is as true in most animal species as it is in humans. Newcomers to the world need guidance and training from those who are more experienced. Adults tend to be the key "modelers" for younger children and then peers take over during the pre-teen and teenage years. Modeling entails demonstrating behaviors, although these may not always be positive. (For example, teens often learn how to smoke by watching their peers—a very negative behavior, yet they tend to do it correctly.) Both adult and peer-modeling are important and powerful forms of instruction supported by a fairly broad base of research.

Self-modeling—watching and learning from our own positive behavior—is the "new kid on the block." Until relatively recently, the only way to conduct self-modeling has been with the use of mirrors. The advent of photography and then motion pictures has given us the platform to conduct self-modeling, but these media, especially the video camera, only came into common use following World War II. Both media were quickly adapted for instructional purposes, but their uses were limited to addressing global topics aimed at a general and large audience.

It was the military and then the sports world that began systematically filming and analyzing videos of particular events as a teaching aid. Individuals or groups could examine videos to assess their own performance and then attempt to improve it. This form of viewing, in which both positive and negative behaviors is shown, is called *self-observation.* The classic example of self-observation is the coach showing films of last week's game. Players view the good, the bad, and the ugly. Much of the emphasis is on learning from mistakes.

Research into self-observation indicates generally positive results; however, there are reports that viewing negative behavior frustrates some people and exacerbates their problems. To return to the sports analogy, players who watch images of mostly negative performances may start to lose any confidence that they might have had. This, in turn, could limit their improvement and lead to even worse performance. Enter self-modeling. If self-modeling were used by the coach, he or she would edit out all the negatives and show only the best performances from the game. This could be done for individuals in the group. For example, a lineman who completes only 40 percent of his blocks correctly could be shown only the good blocks. Although there is no published research on using positive self-modeling in sports, I would predict that results would be better than with self-observation.

Self-observation could be especially problematic for use with children with developmental delays who may already lack confidence. I therefore do not recommend self-observation for individuals with autism or related disorders.

Video Self-Modeling (VSM) Defined

Self-modeling requires one more step than self-observation: editing the video to show only instances when the individual was performing the skill or behavior correctly. It is only recently that editing technology has become available to the general population. This may go a long way in explaining why self-modeling research and application has lagged behind other forms of modeling. Now that researchers are exploring this method, we are finding reasons why self-modeling may take the whole concept of modeling to a higher level.

Peter Dowrick (1983)—a pioneer in the field, now working at the University of Hawaii, Manoa—defined two forms of self-modeling:
1. feedforward, and
2. positive self-review.

Feedforward

In the feedforward method of VSM, a person is shown video of himself performing a new, yet developmentally appropriate behavior. One of the ways I have used feedforward is to capture words spoken by children who are only using one- or two-word utterances. Using video editing software, I extract clips of individual words, resulting in what amounts to a series of word cards on my computer. I then combine the individual words into short sentences. Played back, it sounds like the child is speaking in sentences—a new skill for him.

Feedforward allows children to see themselves as they will probably be some time in the future. Hopefully, this vision of the future serves as a magnet accelerating the growth toward that future. It is important to be very careful not to project too far ahead so that the images represent reasonable expectations for the child.

Positive Self-Review

The second form of VSM defined by Dowrick is positive self-review. This method involves watching videos of oneself to build fluency or proficiency in a skill already learned. I remember watching the platform diving competition in the Sydney Olympics in 2000. Laura

Wilkinson, the U.S. gold medal winner, was being interviewed following her victory and was asked how she prepared for an event. She stated that she watched videos of her best dives that also included images of her coach and parents giving her encouragement. This is positive self-review. Laura already had the skill, but was working to improve it.

Results of self-review tend not to be as dramatic as feedforward. To a large extent, this is because the beginning or baseline rate of behavior tends to be higher than with feedforward; there is less room for improvement. However, with some individuals with autism spectrum or other forms of developmental disabilities, the baseline rate of behaviors is so low that change can be significant. For example, a child with autism may verbally initiate, but only in times of extreme stress or only with one person. Actual initiations are extremely rare, but the capacity is there and even one initiation per week constitutes a baseline rate of performance.

I tend to use the term feedforward when working with emerging behaviors that occur rarely or infrequently and reserve the use of self-review for times when an individual has over 50 percent proficiency on a behavior or performance. Part of the reason my definition may differ somewhat from that of Dowrick's is that I just like the term feedforward. I think it captures the essence of the self-modeling effects.

Rationale for Using VSM with People with Autism Spectrum Disorders

Video self-modeling and its possible effects on mind and behavior are supported by several lines of research. There is also anecdotal support for the method arising out of personal experiences of families who are using similar approaches to teaching their children, as well as testimonials from individuals with autism. I want to address these issues here because the effects seen from using VSM may be a result of a variety of factors that coalesce in the act of viewing a video. Understanding these diverse factors may provide information as to how to maximize effects and explain why, at times, the effects are so strong. I think you will also see that while anyone could benefit from self-modeled instruction, certain groups of people, such as those with autism, might be particularly likely to benefit from it.

I have already touched on the mysterious way that children with autism spectrum disorders accept the two-dimensional TV human

Other Types of Video Modeling

As described above, video modeling in general involves watching only positive examples of a behavior or skill. This book focuses on video self-modeling, in which the individual watches video of himself doing the behavior or skill correctly. You should also know that there are two other alternatives for video modeling: adult and peer modeling. In these forms of modeling, either an adult or a peer is videotaped doing the behavior that the person with disabilities needs to learn.

Within the self-modeling category, the three alternatives of adult, peer, and self-modeling provide a range of possible filming scenarios. Recently, several commercial products have been introduced that use adult and peer modeling and target behaviors common in children with ASD. Autisme was developed in England in the late 1990s. It was designed for older students who would soon be transitioning from school to community. Video examples of how to properly address social situations were embedded into stories that dealt with the same scenarios. This was a good idea, but unfortunately the product is no longer published.

More recently, Carol Gray and Mark Shelley (2007) produced the DVD-based *Storymovie* product that uses both adult and peer models to depict proper ways of handling challenging social situations. It is similar to the written Social Stories that Gray has been using for years to help individuals with autism spectrum disorders. The difference is that instead of reading the Social Stories, the individual watches them being acted out. The set of approximately 25 individual Social Stories costs about $150 for the full version. This price may be prohibitive for some families.

The research into the effects of adult and peer video-modeling on children with autism is very limited. However, the rationales presented in this book concerning why video self-modeling might be so effective with children with autism do have implications for peer and adult modeling. Given the power of the medium and the visual learning styles of many people with autism, it seems that there is good potential for peer and adult modeling to be successful. In many cases, producing a video featuring typically developing peers would be easier to film than one using a child with an autism spectrum disorder, especially when that child is very young or has more severe autism. However, as you'll read below, one researcher (Bandura, 1997) has found that: 1) the more similar somebody is to the model he is watching, the more closely that person will pay attention to the model, and 2) that people are more likely to attempt a skill if they feel confident they can do it. Given these findings, the effects of self-modeling should be greater than for either peer or adult modeling.

while avoiding the real three-dimensional version. It could be that there is no requirement for social interaction attached to the TV figure as there is with Mom, Dad, or teacher. This is a concept addressed and confirmed by Temple Grandin in *Thinking in Pictures*. If this is the case, then video self-modeling, and video in general, may present a particularly potent pathway for teaching these children.

Two families have published works about training children with autism using video as the medium. The Zahinni family in England published the "A–Z Method" on the Internet (the site is no longer available). They did task analyses of academic skills such as math and then created step-by-step videos for each skill. Then they had their child watch them. They reported very good success with their child. Similarly, Liisa Neumann published the book *Video Modeling: A Visual Teaching Method for Children with Autism* in 1999, based on the work she and her husband did with their child with autism. She included scripts and how-to instructions for creating videos. The focus here was on peer modeling, but again, very positive results were noted. Self-modeling takes these ideas one step further by allowing children with autism to be the stars of the video and to be their own models.

Children as Their Own Best Models

The fact that the child serves as his own model in VSM has important implications. Albert Bandura—who developed social learning theory and did extensive research on the role of modeling and self-confidence in learning— carried out extensive studies on the influence of models (1969; 1997). He found that the most effective models were those who had attributes that were most similar to the viewer's. This included such traits as gender, age, race, and, interestingly—ability. The best models were not the paragons of success, but those who were only slightly more advanced than the observer.

These findings indicate two ways that the power of self-modeling might be amplified compared to other forms of modeling. First, it would be impossible to find anyone more similar to the observer than the observer himself. Secondly, and related to the first, when using VSM, the model is identical to the observer in all developmental attributes save one that will be slightly advanced: the behavior selected for video editing. Although Bandura's research focused on peer and adult modeling, in his later writings, he addressed self-modeling as possibly the purest form of modeling.

Boosting Confidence

Another aspect of Bandura's research dealt with self-efficacy or the confidence people feel regarding their ability to successfully carry out a task.

Everybody would fit somewhere on a confidence scale for any given skill. For example, my confidence level is very low for anything to do with music. I am tone deaf and have short, wide fingers. If I were given a guitar and told to learn to play it, I would experience great anxiety and would probably make extremely slow progress. Part of the problem is that my physical and auditory abilities in this area are limited. The other factor working against me is that my self-efficacy is almost nonexistent. I have learned from previous experience that I will not be having fun. I would be the Little Engine That Couldn't. A person's feeling of self-efficacy is often directly related to his success when trying to learn a new skill or improve upon an existing one.

Building self-efficacy is another area in which self-modeling has great potential. When someone views images of himself successfully

If this cello student watches an unedited video of her practice session, it will be self-review. If she watches only the best, error-free segments, it will be self-modeling.

performing a behavior, he has visual evidence that he can do it. To take the Little Engine analogy one step further, it is no longer "I think I can, I think I can." It becomes "I know I can, I know I can—I've seen it." By improving an individual's self-efficacy, we greatly increase chances for success.

We saw this effect vividly at a school connected with the University of Memphis when working with three struggling readers. The three girls were about to be referred for assessment for special education placement. We took passages from their 4th grade readers—which were supposedly two years above their actual reading level—and worked with the students on vocabulary, fluency, and reading with inflection. We then made a video of these students reading very fluently on grade level. The effects were immediate. After school on the first day the girls watched the videos, two of their teachers sought out my graduate assistant to ask what we had done. This was in November and they related that both girls had volunteered to read orally for the first time.

We made another interesting finding when we evaluated the three students in reading. We were tracking their progress with daily probes of reading fluency using their grade level books and had done pretests with standardized tests. Following intervention, their scores on both forms of assessment improved dramatically. We never taught specific skills—just allowed the girls to watch themselves being successful. Simply by building confidence we seemed to have had a great impact on their performance. They seemed to have had an aura of defeatism related to reading that was dispelled by seeing images of success.

Another group of researchers also achieved results indicating that the power in VSM may be more in its ability to convince observers that they can do a skill than in its ability to teach the steps in that skill. A study carried out at the University of Alaska (Gonzales, cited in Dowrick, 1983) examined whether the positive effects of self-modeling resulted from learning skill information or from increasing self-confidence. In this study, the researchers focused on increasing the participants' ability to sink pool (billiard) balls into the pocket. One group of participants was videotaped lining up a shot that was successful and watching the ball fall into the hole. Another group was videotaped using incorrect cue stick angles that resulted in missed shots, but the results were edited to show the balls falling into pockets. Both groups of participants then watched their respective videos. The results were compared to a control group and indicated significant improvement for both treatment groups as compared to control, but no difference between self-modeling groups. As with our study of reading skills discussed above, this study also bolsters the idea that motivational factors rather than skill information may sometimes be the key factor for growth via video self-modeling.

Again, boosting self-efficacy is inherent in self-modeling. We provide visual proof to the individual that something can be done. However, one caveat needs to be emphasized here. The behaviors that you work with via VSM must be developmentally appropriate. If I were shown a video that made it appear I was a great guitar player (which could easily be done with video editing software), it might motivate me for a while, but it could lead to great frustration as I realized that the vision of myself succeeding was an obvious distortion. We must be very careful and realistic in our choice of behaviors to work with. That caveat aside, it is safe to say that Bandura's research and his subsequent theories of social learning provide insight into why self-modeling may produce results for individuals with ASD and other disabilities that transcend the norm.

Capturing and Maintaining Attention

The next factor supporting the use of VSM with individuals with ASD relates to its potential to capture and hold their attention. Using media to attract and hold attention is the major goal of advertising. Many businesses are dependent on their ability to attract a person to their product. The whole advertising industry has grown up around this dependency. Likewise, teachers often seek better ways to attract students' attention to a lesson and to hold their interest. When we instruct teachers on how to write lesson plans, one of the sections is the set. This is usually a short activity prior to the actual instruction designed to motivate and draw students into the lesson. Advertising professionals would call this the hook.

We know that having students pay attention to the relevant instruction and stay on task is key to the success of a lesson, and, accordingly, to student learning. Self-modeling may have several features that both hook and maintain attention. Here we must look at both the medium and the innate abilities of the person who will be viewing the video because both relate to the potential impact that self-modeling may have.

The TV and computer screens act as magnets to many children and young people. As a culture, we spend a good percentage of our waking hours watching TV or sitting at a computer. We watch the programs we prefer, but if programming were different (like all education channels or C-span programs that presently do not have high viewer ratings), I do not think there would be a sharp drop-off in viewing. The medium itself is a powerful attractor.

The TV screen captures an audience early in life. By the age of 3 months, 40 percent of infants in the United States are regular television viewers, and by 2 years, the number increases to 90 percent (Christakis, Zimmerman, DiGiuseppe & McCarty, 2004). Of importance to our discussion is a theory called the moderate-discrepancy hypothesis (Siegler, 1991) that addresses the television content preferred by infants and preschoolers. The theory is remarkably similar to the findings of Bandura related to the best models. Young children pay the most attention to television content that is only moderately different from their own experience and abilities. If it is too simplistic or too complex, interest wanes. Once again we find a rationale for why VSM might be especially effective. Everything a child would see in a self-modeling video would match his or her experiences and abilities, and any differences seen would be "moderate."

Many children with autism spectrum disorders take viewing to an extreme. Some become almost obsessed with specific programs or videos. I just finished a project that required over 200, 15-minute observations in 2 classrooms in a preschool that was comprised of an equal number of children with and without disabilities. Each of these classrooms had a computer center with a single PC. Children were able to choose the computer as a center-time option. Not surprisingly, those with symptoms of autism often chose the computer. However, the behavior I observed when the children were away from the computer was most interesting to me. Often they would be gazing at the screen from long distance, sometimes gravitating back to the center and looking over the shoulders of the children now using it. When the children were working at the computer, I would observe them using expressions and other pragmatic language applications that I never saw in their other day-to-day interactions.

However strong the pull of the screen is, however, a person still must have the ability to attend to it for VSM to be effective. In rare situations that is not possible. On three occasions I used self-modeling and saw no positive results. In each of these cases, attending to the TV was problematic for the observer. Two of these situations involved teens with severe autism and mental retardation (intellectual disabilities). The other was with a two-year-old who was classified as having attention deficit disorder (ADD). I realize that all two-year-olds have some difficulties with attention, but this child actually fit the ADD label. Interestingly, the child repeated everything he said on his video during the time he was viewing the film (we were trying to get him to increase his oral vocabulary and to use these words in simple sentences). He was tuned in to the soundtrack, but he could not keep his eyes on the screen for more than a few seconds. Even though he repeated words he rarely or never used during the intervention sessions, he never used them in other settings.

The ability to attend is essential to learning in general, and to self-modeling specifically. Attention to task is one of the few skills that has been linked to later school success (Duncan et al., 2007). Screen media tend to maximize attention for many people, although very young children and people with disabilities that directly affect attention may have difficulty paying attention to videos. However, only a small percentage of children and students with autism spectrum disorders and other disabilities have this difficulty. For the vast majority, the video screen has great power in attracting attention and holding interest.

Shaping Positive Memories

One last factor that should be considered is how self-modeling can affect memory and how this, in turn, can affect habits that we want to change. Thomas Kehle and his colleagues (2002) addressed the possibilities of using video self-modeling to build new memories after working with children with emotional disturbance. They hypothesized that children who view themselves performing positive, adaptive behaviors would not only have this new memory implanted, but that it also might supplant memories of the inappropriate behavior. If this hypothesis turns out to be true, it would go a long way in explaining: 1) why behavior change is so rapid when using VSM with some individuals, and 2) why VSM can be effective in changing habitual behaviors that have been resistant to other forms of intervention.

I vividly remember working with two nine-year-old children with Asperger's syndrome who had tantrums at least once per day. Their case study will be presented in detail later, but I wanted to address one facet of their reaction to the self-modeling intervention. We noted all situations that triggered the tantrums and then videotaped these two children acting out the situations while exhibiting appropriate behavior. The day after the children watched the tapes, their tantrums almost completely ceased. What was interesting was that the children would often enter into the "aura" that typically marked the onset of the tantrum (scowling, folding arms, tightening of back and neck), but then back off suddenly. Several times one of the children lightly smacked his forehead with his palm and said, "Oops." It was as though the habitual behavior was triggered, but then the adaptive memory quickly followed and overrode it.

Some recent research carried out in England by Caroline Wright and Dave Smith (2009) has suggested that memories implanted by VSM may even be able to affect physiology. They compared the effects of five different strength-training regimens on bicep development. One group of participants did a set of two strenuous exercises three days per week on a curl machine, one group used conventional mental imagery of doing arm curls, while another group worked on the curl machine doing only one set of the same exercise as the first group. This group then watched videos of themselves doing curls for a time equivalent to doing one of the exercise sets. The other two groups consisted of a control that did nothing and one of self-modeling only. After six weeks, it was found that the only groups that gained strength were the physical exercise only and the self-modeling/exercise groups. There was no significant difference between these two groups, although the combined group (VSM and exercise) gained 28 percent in strength and the exercise group gained 25 percent.

More validation needs to be done with this research and it is ongoing; however, in this arm-curl study it was clear that using self-modeling with some exercise allowed participants to develop strength at a rate equal to those doing twice the work. If we can change muscle physiology, it is likely that neural activity can also be manipulated.

Thinking about the potential effects self-modeling may have on shaping memory is tantalizing. In one sense, it has an Orwellian cast to it in that we are shaping how people think. However, we must keep in mind that in VSM we only show positive, adaptive images that are developmentally appropriate. When we work with children, we let them see past obstacles that might be impeding their development and allow them to have a vision of mastery over their own environment.

Putting the Potential Positive Effects of VSM Together

When we look at this range of factors that may add to the effectiveness of VSM, it is interesting to wonder how they affect the observer. Are the factors cumulative in their effects? Does the combination of factors serve to propel self-modeling to a higher plane than peer or adult-modeling? How do these factors affect children with autism and other developmental disabilities? If, in fact, the factors addressed above have a cumulative effect, we may be looking at a very powerful form of instruction.

To date, many of our questions about VSM remain unanswered, as much research still remains to be done. The next section, however, will review some of the most important research findings to date.

Across Behaviors and Ages: An Overview of the Research

This section provides an overview of the research that has been carried out with self-modeling. We will be working from a small sample, but I hope to give you an idea of the state of affairs of research into VSM and also give you some insight into how the research was carried out. Specifically, I urge you to look at how data were collected and how student performance was evaluated. Hopefully, you will be able to put some of this information to use when you start using self-modeling with your child(ren), or at least get ideas about the range of behaviors that might be addressed with VSM.

Before I get into a discussion of the research, here are a few points to keep in mind when reading summaries of research about modeling, or indeed, educational research in general.

First, you should know that in dealing with research on human behavior, there are some unique factors that muddy the waters and make conclusive findings very difficult. The variables that factor into human behavior and performance are so complex that even the most controlled studies cannot approximate the control seen in research in biology or the earth sciences. We must rely on a preponderance of evidence before we can make claims about human behavior, and there are factors at play in the research community that make gathering substantial evidence more difficult.

Second, while it is important to expand our knowledge about human behavior by slightly modifying previous research, it is also important to ensure that results of the original research were valid. This need for originality and the need for replication (repeating research to verify the findings) sometimes are in conflict in the research arena. One thing that is missing from much of education research is replication, and this is the case with self-modeling. There are two main reasons for this. One is that merely replicating a study is frowned on in higher education circles. Doctoral students and researchers in higher education are often required to justify their work by stating how it adds "new knowledge to the field." (I would, however, propose that replicating previous studies and finding similar or conflicting results does add new knowledge to the field.)

The other reason that replication is often lacking in education research is that it is very difficult to replicate a study based on the descriptions found in journals and given the myriad factors that are at play during any study. Each setting and every study participant have inherent differences. This is why it is important to have a critical eye when viewing educational and psychological research. Take nothing at face value. Any given study can be flawed by unforeseen factors. However, as the number of studies dealing with a particular theory or practice grows, we can begin making cautious statements about outcomes. The forest tends to be much more important than the individual trees. I believe we have reached a point in the self-modeling research where we can begin making modest claims about the generic use of self-modeling and some stronger claims about its use with specific groups of individuals, such as those with autism spectrum disorders.

Research into Video Self-Modeling

An overview of the literature reveals 26 studies that have addressed the effects of self-modeling across individuals with a range of ages and disabilities. A summary of these studies is presented in Table 1 on pages 16-19.

The results of these studies give us reason to be optimistic about the potential of video modeling, as the vast majority of studies showed good gains by study participants. You will notice, however, that sample sizes are relatively small and many used a single-subject design (which is addressed below). In a review of studies conducted by Caryl Hitchcock, Peter Dowrick, and Mary Anne Prater, they found that just over 200 subjects had participated in published research. Monica Delano (2007) focused on autism in a review of all video modeling methods, including adult, peer, and self. She found 19 such studies, 5 of which dealt with self-modeling. Scott Bellini and Jennifer Akullian (2007) found 8 studies that evaluated VSM use with individuals with autism.

Although the numbers of studies are small, they are growing and are being supported by reports from school districts and agencies that have been using the method successfully with their students. Findings across studies seem to indicate that using video self-modeling does lead to the generalization of taught skills and that the maintenance of skills is very strong.

Single Subject Designs: Understanding Research Models and Terminology

In looking over Table 1, you probably noticed that many of the studies were "single subject" and/or "across multiple baselines" in design. What do these terms mean?

The most prevalent design used in studying VSM is single subject with multiple baselines. The "single subject" part of this design

Table 1 | Research Studies That Have Addressed Video Self-Modelir

Authors	Design	Participants
Bray & Kehle (1996)	Multiple baseline across persons	3 adolescent males
Buggey (1995)	Multiple baseline across persons	3 students w/ language delays
Buggey (2005)	Multiple baseline across behaviors and persons	5 students; 5-12 yr-olds w/ ASD
Buggey, Toombs, Gardener, & Cervetti (1999)	Multiple baseline across persons	3 students w/ autism ages 9—11
Creer & Miklich (1970)	Case study	10-yr-old male
Davis (2004)	Pretest-posttest	2 female adolescents With dev. disabilities
Decker (2001)	Multiple baseline across persons	9 students in Special Education ages 8-12
Dowrick (1983)	Case study	6-yr-old female
Dowrick & Dove (1980)	Multiple baseline across persons	3 children
Dowrick & Ward (1997)	Single subject	1 adult w/ cognitive disability
Greenberg, Buggey, & Bond (2003)	Multiple baseline across persons	3 fourth graders
Haarman & Greelis (1982)	Case study Multiple baseline	15-yr-old female
Hartley, Bray, & Kehle (1998)	Multiple baseline across persons	3 second graders
Hepting & Goldstein (1992)	Multiple baseline across persons	4 preschool children
Hitchcock, Prater, & Dowrick (2004)	Multiple baseline across persons	4 first graders w/ reading disabilities

Dependent Variable (the behavior that researchers tried to change)	Outcome
Stuttering	Much less stuttering in social situations. Results maintained for 2 of the 3 in a two-year follow-up
Use of "to be" verbs	Rapid and generalized use of verbs
Pushing, language tantrums, social interactions	Rapid improvement across all behaviors and students
Responding to questions	Doubling of response rates across all students
Noncompliant behaviors	Reduction in target behaviors
On-task behavior	Rapid Improvement in on-task behavior; Off-task behaviors dropped by 50%
Oral reading fluency	VSM results superior to peer modeling, and control
Stepping over obstacles	Improvement plus generalization
Swimming skills	Improvement
Inappropriate sexual behavior	Rapid, generalized improvement
Oral reading fluency & reading self-efficacy	Immediate improvement in fluency Improved scores in self-efficacy
Grammatical and contextual language use	Improvement
Classroom Participation	Improvement
Requesting behaviors	Improvement only when VSM delivered in classroom
Oral reading fluency	VSM and tutoring produced greater gains than tutoring alone

(continued on next page)

(continued from previous page)

Authors	Design	Participants
Hosford & Brown (1976)	Multiple baseline with withdrawal	1 adult
Kahn, Kehle, Jenson, & Clark (1990)	pretest-posttest	68 children ages 10-14
Kehle, Madaus, Baratta, & Bray (1998)	Single-case A-B	3 children
McCurdy & Shapiro (1988)	Multiple baseline across persons	3 children, mean age 9.11
Meharg & Lipsker (1991)	Multiple baseline across persons	4 parent—child dyads
Miklich, Chida, & Danker-Brown (1977)	Multiple baseline	12 children ages 7-12
Pigott & Gonzales (1987)	Case study Multiple baseline	9-yr-old male
Schunk & Hanson (1989)	Pretest-posttest	48 children ages 9-13
Wert & Neisworth (2003)	Multiple baseline across persons	4 preschoolers w/ autism
Wright & Smith (in press)	pretest-posttest	50 college students

is quite simple. It does not mean that you only have one person in the study. Rather, you look at one child at a time rather than evaluating group performance.

You begin by collecting data on each child's performance prior to starting any intervention and chart these on a graph with an x and y axis. This is because you must know this beginning rate (referred

Dependent Variable	Outcome
Self-monitoring of assertive behaviors	Client-rated improvement
Self-ratings of depression	VSM intervention was significantly better than control in reducing depression and increasing self-esteem ratings
Selective mutism	VSM as part of a multi-component intervention package resulted in complete cessation of selective mutism
Disruptive behaviors	2 of 3 subjects showed greater improvement during VSM compared to peer-modeling
3 parent behaviors	No improvement until parents were informed that videotapes exhibited positive behaviors
Bed-making	Statistically significant improvement
Volunteering answers and responding to direct questions	Improvement to equivalency with peers
Fraction skills and self-efficacy	VSM and peer-modeling were equally effective and significantly better than control
Spontaneous requesting	Large increase in requesting behaviors
Bicep strength	Combination of VSM/exercise equivalent to exercise only

to as baseline) in order to make comparisons with later performance. Typically the x axis on the chart is a measure of time, either in number of days or observation sessions. The y axis has a measure of what you are trying to change (e.g., number of words spoken, duration of tantrums). Every data point, be it from an observation session or a total of events for a day, is charted.

There are usually two and often three phases of a single subject design:

a. Baseline (the rate, frequency, or duration of behaviors **prior** to intervention);

b. Intervention (the rate, frequency, or duration of behaviors **during** treatment); and

c. Maintenance or follow-up (the rate, frequency, or duration of behaviors **after** treatment is withdrawn).

A major problem with studies that use small numbers of participants is that it is very hard to ensure that it is the intervention you introduce that is causing the change. Maybe the child experienced something in class or on TV that caused the change. Maybe it was natural maturation that caused a behavior to decrease. Maturation with very young children is an especially hard variable to control. The multiple-baseline concept is designed to solve this problem. A more descriptive name for this method might be the staggered start design.

Let's say you are working with a child on three behaviors—one related to language, one to eating different foods, and one to social initiations. You start collecting baseline data on all three behaviors, but then you only use the intervention (in our case, a self-modeling video) on the first behavior. When you see a change, you introduce the intervention on the second skill. Likewise, intervention starts on skill 3 when you see a change in behavior 2. A visual inspection of the graph will tell you whether the changes occurred at the same time that the intervention was introduced. If the improvement corresponds to the time you introduced the intervention, then you can be fairly certain that it was causing the change.

A design in which one child participates in the study and you examine several behaviors is called a multiple-baseline design *across behaviors*. The same concept can be applied when working with the same behavior with multiple students. You start collecting baseline data on all children simultaneously. You then introduce an intervention with child 1 while continuing to collect baseline data for the others. When a change is seen in child 1, you can start the intervention with child 2, and so on. This method is logically termed a multiple-baseline design *across persons*. The staggering of starts helps build validity for the findings. A sample of the results from a multiple-baseline design across persons is presented in Figure 1-1.

This single-subject design is the only type of research design that will be discussed in any depth in this section. We have emphasized

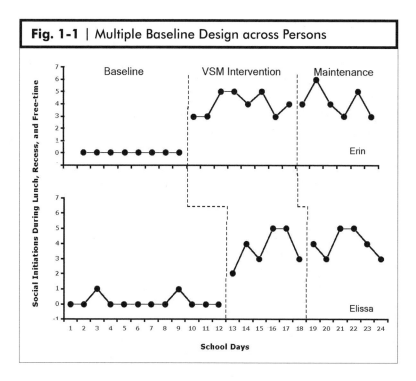

Fig. 1-1 | Multiple Baseline Design across Persons

single subject designs because they have relevance for any data collection that you might do at home or school to evaluate the efficacy of VSM. The idea of establishing the baseline rate of performance and then charting gains (or lack of gains) allows you to evaluate whether VSM is having an effect. In Chapter 3 we will cover assessments in greater detail. Now let us turn our attention to what researchers have found when investigating VSM.

What Skills and Behaviors Can Be Taught through VSM?

This section will provide more detail about some of the studies listed in Table 1 with an emphasis on what the researchers attempted to teach through video self-modeling and how effective their interventions were.

Improving Behavior
Improving Aggressive and Inappropriate Behaviors. The first reported educational application of VSM appeared in 1970 (Creer

& Miklich, 1970). This was a case study of a 10-year-old boy who was considered aggressive and exhibited age-inappropriate behaviors. The goal was to reduce the boy's negative behaviors. The child was videotaped during a role-playing session in which he was asked to model both his appropriate and inappropriate behaviors. Two weeks following the videotaping, the boy began watching the videotape with only positive behaviors 5 minutes daily for 2 weeks. This resulted in a marked improvement in his behavior. For the next 2 weeks the boy watched the videos with the negative behaviors, and his inappropriate behaviors returned to a level similar to that before the intervention. Subsequently, he again watched the positive behavior tape, which led to an improvement in his behaviors that he maintained over 6 months.

Improving Behavior in Children with AD/HD. M. A. Wolters-dorf (1992) employed VSM in a multiple-baseline design across behaviors to analyze changes in noncompliant and disruptive behaviors with a 6-year-old boy diagnosed as having attention-deficit/hyperactivity disorder (AD/HD). As in all cases of VSM intervention, videotapes of the child were edited to show only positive examples of the forms of behavior that the researcher were trying to change. Both of the boy's target behaviors responded positively to treatment via VSM.

Woltersdorf (1992) then expanded on the previous study by investigating the effectiveness of VSM with four boys between the ages of 9 and 10 years who were diagnosed as having AD/HD. The dependent variables (what you want to change) included fidgeting, distractibility, vocalizations, and poor math performance. All four boys experienced statistically significant reductions in all the behaviors, plus gains in math performance.

Improving Disruptive Behavior. In 1988, B. L. McCurdy and E. S. Shapiro reported on a study they had done to compare the effectiveness of peer- vs. self-modeling. In this study, researchers used video modeling in conjunction with a school-wide reward system to try to reduce the disruptive behaviors of five students. These students attended a school for children with social and emotional disturbances and had a mean age of 9 years and 11 months. All of the students in the study watched self-modeling videos at some stage in the study, and four of the five students also watched peer-modeling videos showing a 12-year-old student behaving appropriately.

The authors reported that their findings exhibited a range of effectiveness. The student who only watched self-modeling videos made gradual but consistent improvement in his behavior. Two of the four students who saw both peer- and self-modeling videos reduced their disruptive behavior after watching both types of videos, but made more improvement after watching the self-modeling videos. And two of the students did not respond to either peer- or self-modeling treatments. It is difficult to determine whether the results of this study were more affected by student characteristics, the independent variables, or methodology. However, the study appears to support the efficacy of VSM somewhat, while indicating that it may not work for everyone.

Improving Motor Skills

Peter Dowrick, who is often considered the "Dean of Self-Modeling," carried out a study in the early 1970s that became a benchmark for other studies. The study participant was a young girl named Shirley who had cerebral palsy. Shirley could walk in a shuffling manner, but could not lift her legs to step over objects. Dowrick filmed Shirley navigating an obstacle course of 1-inch wooden blocks. Attendants were giving her physical assistance to lift her legs as she walked. The filming focused on Shirley's face and feet so that neither the attendants nor any signs of their physical assistance were visible. The day Shirley watched her video, she successfully navigated the obstacle course without assistance. Even more impressively, when taken outside, she successfully stepped off and onto curbs and walked up stairs. It is important to note that independently lifting her legs was part of Shirley's physical therapy plan and that the professionals working with her had agreed that she could accomplish this skill.

Dowrick followed up his study of Shirley with another study involving children with physical disabilities. In 1980, he and Cynthia Dove applied VSM to teaching swimming skills to children with spina bifida. They broke down the swimming skills into a series of 35 separate behaviors. This enabled them to teach sequential steps as children demonstrated the acquisition of prerequisite skills. Three children were followed during the study and data were recorded using a multiple-baseline design. Two of the children participated in only one stage of the study, while a third was observed through a succession of four self-modeling tapes that represented slightly more difficult levels of performance. The scoring was done on an author-made measure of swimming skills that grouped the 35 swimming skills into 4 categories based on difficulty. Videotapes were made of children demonstrating skills from a category in which they could perform some, but not all, of the skills.

Following initiation of VSM, each participant's swimming performance improved and the improvements were maintained throughout the treatment stage. The child who was shown successive tapes with increased difficulty levels continued to make progress. A follow-up 6 weeks after the completion of the first VSM phase showed that the child had maintained the new behaviors.

Based on Dowrick's and Dove's success in using VSM for teaching successively difficult skills, it appears that VSM has the potential for being an important intervention in teaching developmental skills in preschool programs.

Improving Mood and Self-Esteem

Several studies have attempted to compare VSM with other forms of intervention. One study (Kahn, Kehle, Jenson, & Clark, 1990) examined the relative effects of VSM, relaxation, and cognitive behavioral treatment with 68 depressed middle-school students. The VSM group was informed of the intent of the study and was instructed to behave in a manner that was incompatible with typical depressed behavior such as maintaining appropriate eye contact, smiling, using good posture, and making positive statements about themselves and their environment. The students were filmed and then given 3-minute videos that they watched twice weekly for 6 to 8 weeks.

The results showed significant improvement in a measure of self-esteem and significant decreases in depression for all of the treatment groups when compared to a control group that did not receive any treatment. The results were maintained in a one-month follow-up analysis and were validated by parent ratings of their child's progress during treatment.

Improving Social and Language Skills

Since social skills and language skills are a significant area of difficulty for people on the autism spectrum, research into how VSM can improve these skills is especially relevant for this book. To date, very few studies have been conducted on using VSM to help individuals with ASD with language and communication skills, but what studies have been done are described below. In addition, some studies on other individuals and groups have produced promising results, also discussed below.

The areas of speech and language development seem a natural fit for VSM. Therapists have long used mirrors to show clients the proper mouth formations for certain sounds and this in itself is a form of self-modeling. Furthermore, many children can imitate sounds and words that they don't typically use, making for a situation that facilitates filming.

Improving Use of Expressive Language in a Stressful Environment. A combination of VSM and self-monitoring was adapted by H. Edmund Pigott and Frank Gonzales (1987) to effectively treat a 9-year-old boy described as being electively mute. Since entering school four years prior to the study, the child had been extremely shy and socially withdrawn, and did not respond to direct questions or initiate verbal interactions while at school. These behaviors were not as noticeable when family members were present.

The authors chose responding to direct questions and volunteering answers as the target behaviors. The child had a zero response rate in the classroom during the baseline phase of the study. Videotaping was done in the classroom with the boy's parents and brother present. To obtain responses not given by the child and to increase his voice volume on the tape, the mother asked some questions after class and the responses were later edited into the tape of the classroom scene. During the classroom videotaping with the parents present, the child responded to 70 percent of the questions posed by his teacher. Soon afterwards, when a classroom session was observed without family present, the boy's responses dropped to 10 percent. The parents were given the tape and asked to have their son watch it each morning before coming to school.

A similar strategy was applied to taping the boy volunteering to answer questions. Baseline for this behavior was also zero. He volunteered 7 times during the classroom videotaping with his family present, but he volunteered only once in a subsequent observation. Once again, the researchers did some creative editing of the video and placed the responses when the parents were present into the context of the classroom. The videos made it appear that the boy was responding during regular classes.

Once the boy began to watch the videos, his responses to direct questions and his rate of volunteering rose dramatically. Over the course of the study, he continued responding to direct questions to the point that he was responding at the same rate as his peers. However, his initial gains in volunteering had completely disappeared by the tenth observation period following intervention. The child was then taught to self-monitor his volunteering. Each time he volunteered in class, he was allowed to give himself a specified reward. Six months later, the boy was continuing to volunteer in class and was using other positive social behaviors.

Increasing Verbal Responding and Initiation. Recently, I completed a study involving one preschool boy with autism using a multiple baseline design across three behaviors: pushing, verbal responding, and initiating conversation without prompting (Buggey, 2005).

The boy's pushing behavior virtually ceased after he viewed a videotape showing his own positive interactions and appropriate touching. He was shown using substitute behaviors such as an appropriate hug, complying with teacher requests, and playing nicely while a trailer to the video pointed out that "this is the nice way to play with friends."

The boy's responses to questions also significantly improved after he viewed the video. The video contained edited sentences made up of individual words spliced together (see Chapter 3) using computer editing software. The video also pictured classmates posing questions to the child which fit the responses that had been spliced together for him. For example, the student's sentence "I go home" was preceded by "What do you do after school?" asked by a classmate.

Despite the student's gains in making verbal responses, he made only limited improvement in initiating conversation at first. When I reexamined the tape, I decided that the back-and-forth exchanges might be distracting, so I made a second tape that eliminated most of the questions. After the boy viewed this new tape, his level of initiations rose sharply. I concluded that having the child as the sole star provided the best results, at least in this situation. The presence of his peers may have served as distractions.

Making Requests. In another study of preschoolers, Nancy Hepting and Howard Goldstein (1996) set out to find out whether VSM could: 1) promote spontaneous use of more advanced linguistic structures such as requests, and 2) help students generalize the new requesting skill across classroom activities.

Hepting and Goldstein prompted four preschool students to request objects during snack time and play time. Videos were then produced showing each child making requests with the adult prompt eliminated. Although the children soon began making requests in the quiet room where they had been videotaped, they had difficulty generalizing this skill to the preschool classroom. With the help of additional prompting and praise from peers, three of the children eventually began to consistently request things in the classroom. (The fourth child dropped out of the study.)

One of the factors that may have affected the results in this study was the relatively short length of the VSM movie. This is an area where research is needed. Although Peter Dowrick reports that videos longer than 2 ½ minutes show no increase in effectiveness compared to those of 4 to 5-minutes length, we have no idea of the minimum time requirement.

Increasing Social Interactions. Recently, three researchers (Bellini, Akullian, and Hopf, 2007) explored the possibilities of using VSM to train children with autism spectrum disorders to interact with peers in their preschool. The authors noted that techniques typically used to promote interactions such as setting up a buddy system or role-playing had not worked with these children. The authors worked with two preschool children with ASD who had not responded to other interventions. They created videos depicting the children in situations that made them appear to be interacting verbally and physically with their peers. After four weeks of intervention, both children showed dramatic improvements in the number and quality of their interactions with classmates.

We recently completed a similar study at the Siskin Children's Institute. In the spring of 2007, we set up a buddy system in which children with and without disabilities were paired for transitions, center time, and other activities throughout the day (Buggey, Kirkman, and Hoomes, submitted). We also had the teachers read stories to the children and then follow up with questions and role-playing involving helping one another. The rate of unprompted interactions in free-play time increased 240 percent for children with disabilities other than ASD. For those six children with ASD, there were no changes in their interactions with peers and vice versa.

We followed up with four of these children with ASD in the spring of 2008. They continued their tendencies to avoid social contact in all settings. For each child, we made a new self-modeling video, targeting both physical interactions (touch, joining in with groups, etc.) and verbal interactions. We had several typically developing peers serve as "co-stars" and instructed them in what to do with the child with ASD. For example, we pushed them down a double slide simultaneously and had them hold hands with a classmate as they were transitioning onto the playground. Even if the children with ASD rejected the hand in theirs after a short time, we still had footage that we could use where they were holding hands. Because we had data collected over a full year prior to starting the VSM intervention in this study, we had very strong confidence in our baseline data—which was close to zero incidences of appropriate social interactions for all four children.

With the first two children, results were immediate and striking. Not only did their social interactions increase, but their behavior changed in other ways. Their ritualistic behaviors decreased, while their interactions with adults and their range of activities increased. (One child would not usually use the slide, but we convinced him to give it a try for the video. He came down with arms and legs braking his speed and he only made it two-thirds of the way down. However, within a few days of watching his video, he was using slides and even began to swing for the first time.) The fourth child made modest gains, but compared to baseline they were significant. She increased from a baseline of zero interactions during fifteen-minute observation periods to almost three. The third child in our study made no gains at all. Like the other children, he enjoyed watching his video and paid close attention. We are unsure why he did not show improvement.

These last two studies underscore the fact that children with autism spectrum disorders do not respond well to many mainstream teaching methods and that alternatives must be explored. It also seems to indicate that VSM may work where other methods have not.

Improving Academic Skills

Mathematics. Dale Schunk and Antoinette Hanson (1989) conducted a series of three experiments in an attempt to compare VSM to other forms of intervention and to learn how best to administer the treatment. In experiment 1, VSM, peer-modeling, a combination of peer-modeling and VSM, and a control group were compared to determine the effects these interventions had on children's fraction problem-solving skills and self-efficacy (child's perception of his/her ability) ratings. Forty-eight children ranging in age from 9 years, 3 months, to 12 years, 11 months, participated in the study and were randomly assigned to one of the four groups.

Each group received an identical videotape instruction course in fraction problem solving for forty-five minutes over six days. The peer-modeling and the peer and VSM groups also viewed a videotape of three children and a teacher solving fraction problems. All children were videotaped individually after the third problem-solving session, but only the self-modeling and self-plus peer-modeling groups were allowed to view their tapes following instructional sessions. Testing showed that all groups improved their skills and only the control group failed to make significant gains in self-efficacy. No significant differences were found among the modeling groups on any measure. The authors concluded that self-modeling and peer modeling were equally potent in improving skill development and the children's perceptions of their ability.

In experiment 2, the authors sought to determine whether the timing of the self-modeling intervention (early or late in the instructional program) was significant. They had some children begin watching self-modeling videos of fraction problem solving after two of the six instructional sessions, while other children only began watching the videos after four sessions. The researchers found that both groups made significant, comparable gains both in solving fraction problems and in self-efficacy compared to a control group that didn't watch any self-modeling videos.

The third experiment explored the question of whether it was any more effective for children to watch self-modeling videos in which they demonstrated mastery of skills than it was to observe self-modeling videos in which they were just making progress toward skill development. At the end of the study, the researchers found that both groups of children who watched self-modeling videos had made significant gains in their math skills, and that there was no significant difference in the progress the two groups made.

The findings of these studies indicate that VSM can be an effective intervention to enhance mathematics instruction—at least for some groups of children.

Reading. Earlier in the chapter, I discussed a small VSM study that helped several fourth grade girls become more confident in their reading skills and subsequently improve their skills to grade level. Peter Dowrick has been involved in a similar effort, but on a larger scale. With the help of a federal grant, he and some colleagues have piloted the Actual Community Empowerment (ACE) Reading Program in Philadelphia and Hawaii (Dowrick, Kim-Rupnow, & Power, 2006). This program targets children with disabilities and those who are at-risk for reading failure.

The program is basically an after-school program built around a solid, balanced reading program and parent and community involvement. Because many of these children have developed negative attitudes toward reading after years of failure and frustration, building up their self-confidence became a major goal. A key to accomplishing this has been the use of VSM. Once again, very positive results are reported, with 90 percent of participants showing marked improvement in their reading skills after viewing self-modeling videos. While it is not possible to attribute all of the gains to VSM when it is embedded into a broader curriculum package, the administrators of ACE feel that VSM plays a strong part in improving self-confidence, which, in turn, contributes highly to reading success.

In the words of the grant director, "ACE enhances skill mastery and self-efficiency enhanced by video self-modeling (feedfoward) that produces images of success beyond the child's current capability." ACE also has a website with downloadable material at: http://www.creating-futures.org/literacy/ace.

Vocational Skills

One of the few studies that dealt with using VSM with older people was carried out by Peter Dowrick and Marie Hood (1981). They compared the effectiveness of using VSM vs. a behavioral approach involving cash incentives to improve production rates at a sheltered workshop for adults with disabilities. Eighteen participants, ranging in age from 17 to 30, were rated according to their level of work ability and then placed in three equivalent groups. These three groups were then randomly assigned to one of the three treatment groups: self-modeling, points and cash rewards, and control.

A unique feature of the VSM intervention in this study was that the videotapes of individuals at work were combined and then shown to the group as a whole. Participants were called together in the middle of the workday to view the tapes. No comments were made about progress and no form of reinforcement was given. The tape lasted five minutes with each person featured for one minute on the tape. The tapes were edited so each person was shown completing work at approximately six times his actual base rate. Participants in the points and cash reward group were awarded one point for each 10 percent increase in productivity over their baseline rates. The control group met with an experimenter each day to check on hours worked and their productivity, and one extra minute was spent discussing work in general. Thus, every member of the study received one to two minutes of attention daily from an experimenter.

The change in behavior was measured by the percentage change in production between baseline and post-intervention phases. The adults in the VSM and cash incentive groups increased their production by 15 percent and 3 percent, respectively, while the adults in the control group decreased production by 3 percent. Dowrick and Hood attributed most of the gains in production to self-modeling. The increases of the self-modeling group tend to justify the treatment as a low cost, unobtrusive method for improving worker production—at least in a sheltered workshop setting for workers with disabilities.

Transition Skills

In the federally funded Video Futures Project at the University of Alaska–Anchorage, students with disabilities and their families were involved in futures planning as part of their transition program in high school. A team devised a map for each student related to hoped-for outcomes after leaving school. This map became the equivalent to a storyboard and the future situations were set up as simulations in their natural settings. For example, if independent apartment living was a particular student's goal, the student was filmed in an apartment doing activities such as cooking, cleaning, and watching TV. The project participants also enacted and videotaped similar activities related to career skills. Members of the Video Futures Project staff reported very positive outcomes for their participants.

The Video Futures Project in the Center for Human Development at UA-A maintains a website and offers a kit online with videos and literature about their project. There is a fee for this and the technology they used is a bit dated. Nonetheless, it is a great resource. Found at: http://www.alaskachd.org/products/video_futuresj/index.html.

How Early Can You Use VSM?

One area that has not been investigated in detail is the earliest age at which self-modeling is likely to be successful. What little research has been done, however, seems to indicate that the keys are:

1. The child can recognize himself in a mirror or on screen.
2. The child has the attention span to watch a short video.

A simple test for self-recognition is to watch the child's reaction to viewing himself either in a mirror or in a reversed viewfinder of a camcorder.

Self-Recognition Abilities

The development of self-recognition seems to occur between 18–24 months (Lewis & Brooks-Gunn, 1979) for typically developing children, and this age may serve as the lower limit for self-modeling. This time in a child's life also marks the beginning of spoken language, and for children with delayed language, the earlier the intervention the better. It is important that we understand the limitations of VSM relative to the age of the child.

One of my graduate students, Grace Hoomes, and I carried out an informal experiment to gain insight into the age at which children can begin to recognize themselves on screen. The Siskin Children's Institute has three early intervention classes grouped by ages. The first classroom has children ages birth to 1; the second, 1 to 2; and the third, 2 to 3. All of these rooms had children with developmental delays as well as those who were typically developing. We took a camcorder into each of the classrooms and allowed the children to view themselves by turning the view screen around. We had no sign of self-recognition in classroom one. In classroom two, only one child seemed to recognize that it was him in the camera. A child with Down syndrome started making faces and kissed the screen. However, when we moved to the classroom with children over age 2, there was almost universal reaction. My graduate assistant and I joked about discovering the "tongue test" of self-recognition. If the children stuck out their tongues and made faces, it was clear evidence they knew they were viewing themselves.

Another interesting aspect of this little experiment was that the reactions toward the camera seemed consistent between children with and without developmental delays. Still, how developmental delays affect self-recognition, and by association, self-modeling, is another area where research is needed.

Attention Span

To date, there has been no research conducted specifically to determine how long an attention span a child needs in order to benefit from VSM. However, I have done some informal studies that may cast some light on this issue.

I conducted several studies with preschoolers who ranged in age from 2 ½ to 5 years (Buggey 1995, 1996, 2005). The first of these studies, my dissertation, was addressed in the last chapter. I subsequently worked with even younger children, focusing on a boy with attention problems who was 2 ½ and a girl with Down syndrome who had just turned 3. Language was the focus of the study with increasing the average spoken sentence length as the specific target. We videotaped the children imitating sentences that were one and two words longer than their average utterance and then had them watch the video.

The child with Down syndrome made good gains, but the child with the attention problems did not. Interestingly, the girl with Down syndrome sat silently and raptly while watching her video, while the boy verbally imitated everything he said in the video, but attended little to the TV. The results with the boy suggest that the ability to attend to the images in the video and not just the audio is an important factor for success.

Where Do We Go from Here?

This review of the literature gives some idea of the range of behaviors, ages, and types of disabilities that have been addressed by researchers studying the uses of video self-modeling. Although the number of studies is relatively small, the breadth of behaviors and skills addressed is not. It is heartening to see how many more studies have addressed VSM in recent years. I have also read several good dissertations that have yet to be published that should add to our knowledge base. Several of these focus on children with autism.

Although we must be cautious about claims for video self-modeling, it seems safe to say that this technique has great promise and that children with autism spectrum disorders and other developmental disabilities that affect cognitive, social, and language skills may be especially predisposed to treatment effects.

That said, there is still much research to do concerning VSM. There are still more questions than answers. In particular, we need to better understand the thresholds for use of VSM in terms of age and extent of cognitive impairments. We know little about how the actual content and structure of the video affects the viewer other than that a video lasting 2 to 3 minutes seems to produce optimum results and that the use of peers might sometimes be distracting. Would background music help hold attention or serve as a distractor and might the effect be related to age or type of disability? It seems clear that VSM can serve as a great motivator by building positive self-efficacy, but to what extent can we actually teach new skills? A related question would be how far can we go with teaching sequential skills? Would observers tire of watching themselves, decreasing effectiveness? What is the limit for showing skills beyond the child's present ability (how far is too far)?

What are the actual factors that make video so attractive to people with autism and can we take advantage of these to create video programming to better educate them? If, as Temple Grandin suggests, it is the absence of social requirements when watching TV that makes videos so effective, what does this tell us about the social defenses used by students with autism when faced with a real person? Are there ways to limit the social requirements or obligations when teaching children with autism so that we can maximize the impact of direct instruction?

These and many other questions need to be addressed in future research. Part of the companion website for this book will be dedicated to collecting reports from parents and educators about their results and experiences with self-modeling. Hopefully, we can start to answer some of these questions with the help of parents and educators as a supplement to the work of researchers.

The possible applications of VSM are only limited by one's imagination and the ability to master the process and technology. As the necessary technology becomes more widely accessible and more user-friendly, I hope that self-modeling will become a mainstream instructional method that, in turn, will lead to a greater interest in research.

2 | The Process: From Buying Equipment to Watching the Completed Video

Many families today already have the equipment necessary to create a self-modeling tape. According to the U.S. Census Bureau, 99 percent of American households have a color TV, 35 percent own a personal computer, 20 percent have either a camcorder, digital camera with video capacity, or another form of video recording device, and there are over 120,000,000 VCRs in the United States. The minimal technology requirements to produce a self-modeling video are a camcorder and a VCR, although there is a way to use self-modeling with just a regular camera. In this chapter I will walk you through the process of procuring the necessary equipment, planning, filming, and editing the self-modeling videos.

The Equipment

Still Photos and Visual Schedules

Probably the simplest form of self-modeling can be accomplished using still photos. *Graphic organizers* and *visual schedules* are often used to provide visual prompts to children who have difficulty with organization. Visual schedules are in one sense a form of storyboard that illustrates the steps to a more complex task or that shows a sequence of events in chronological order. The steps in the task are typically represented in written format or with picture symbols. For example, the steps

in tooth brushing might be illustrated with line drawings or photos, or with written descriptions such as "Open toothpaste cap"; "Squeeze toothpaste onto toothbrush."

Often times a child can interact with the organizer by checking off when each step in a task is done or by removing a picture symbol that is Velcroed onto a board. The self-modeling version of a visual schedule/graphic organizer would use photos of the child successfully participating in each step of the task.

There is a good deal of research supporting the use of visual schedules with children on the autism spectrum. There is also some evidence that using the child's image adds to the effectiveness of the method (Kimball, Kinney, Taylor, & Stromer, 2003). Jonathan Kimball and his colleagues (Kimball, Kinney, Taylor, & Stromer, 2004) took this idea a step further by using videos of the children acting out the steps of their visual schedules for moving among centers during the day rather than still photos. The children then watched the videotaped steps on a computer prior to the activity. The researchers found this method to be very effective.

The only equipment needed for creating photo visual schedules is a camera and some way of making a hard copy of the photograph. If you have a nondigital camera, you can simply take film to be developed at a drug store. A digital camera allows you to upload images to a computer almost immediately and you can have the images ready in a matter of minutes.

Regular printing paper will work for making the prints, but card stock is better. It will stand up to more use. Laminating the photos or putting them in plastic pockets will add to the durability. The best paper to use is photographic paper designed for use with a printer. The image will be much sharper. This paper is much more expensive than the other two mentioned above; thus, you will want to arrange as many images as possible on one sheet. You can do this by arranging multiple images on a scanner, if available. All photo editing software will also allow you to cut and paste various images onto one photograph. A photo measuring 3 x 3 inches will work fine as part of the visual schedule.

Once you have printed out the images, you can tape Velcro onto the back of the photos and place them in order on a long Velcro strip that is accessible to the child. A common visual schedule used by younger children is a series of possible activities in the classroom that the child can choose from (e.g., reading center, dress-up center, block area). Photos can be taken of the child in that area. For bathroom requests, we take a picture of the child standing next to the toilet. If you are doing the steps in a task such as tooth brushing, you take a photo of the child doing each step.

Some children will need hand-over-hand guidance to do the task. In this case, try to take images right after the prompter's hands, or any other part of his or her body, are removed from view. This may take several attempts, but if at all possible, you want to illustrate the child doing the task independently. An example of a visual schedule of this nature is shown above. The schedule could have a written description of the activity alongside the photo or, if the child does not read, simply numbering the steps would suffice.

Video Self-modeling

There are two main formats for creating self-modeling videos:

a. Camcorder to VCR (or DVD recorder to VHS tape or DVD), and

b. Camcorder to computer to VHS tape or DVD.

With the advent of video editing software for the Mac and PC, the second method is not much harder than the VCR method. Actually, once you become familiar with the software, this method is easier than the VCR-Camcorder method. The second method results in a more professional-looking video.

Equipment Needed to Make Videotapes with a VCR or DVD recorder

To use your VCR to make videos that you can play on your VCR, you need:

1. A camcorder that you can connect to your TV or VCR to play back videos you have recorded
2. Videocassette tapes
3. A VCR capable of recording and playing back videocassette tapes

While VCRs work fine for producing basic videos that can be used in self-modeling, the VHS videocassette is fast becoming obsolete and does not have the quality of digital products. However, the camcorder-VCR combination is available to more households than any other type of video recording equipment and is still commonly found in schools. It provides a very easy format for viewing, editing, and producing VSM tapes.

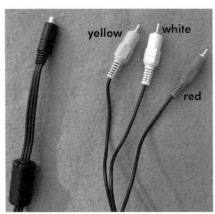

An audio/visual cable used to connect a camcorder to a VCR

To use this method of making a self-modeling video, you also need a camcorder that you can connect to the VCR. Just make sure the camcorder has a VCR mode. Almost all camcorders will have 3 modes: off; camera; and VCR. Only older models will not have these features.

Camcorders come with an audio/visual cable like the one shown in the photo on page 40. This connects directly from the camera to the VCR and all one has to do is match the colors of the cords to the audio and video connectors in the front or the back of the VCR. Yellow is for the video cable and white and red are for the audio.

Once you have filmed your child or student with the camcorder as described later in the chapter, the next step is to transfer the video to a videocassette tape. Turn on the VCR, hit the "record" and "pause" buttons, turn on the camcorder, set to "playback" or "VCR" and you are ready to transfer video onto the VHS tape. See the section on "Editing" below for more information about the transferring process.

Equipment Needed to Make DVDs with DVD Recorder and/or a Computer

To use the **Camcorder/VCR** method of making self-modeling videos, you need, at a minimum:
1. Camcorder;
2. Connector cable;
3. VCR/TV (DVD recorder/player can substitute for VCR)
4. Blank VHS tape

To use the **Camcorder/Computer** method, you need:
1. Camcorder;
2. Connector cable (a USB is OK but a FireWire is better);
3. Video editing software;
4. Blank DVD.

Both methods require that the camcorder have either a blank mini-DVD tape or mini-DVD disk.

DVDs are fast supplanting all other forms of recording and playback media, and they have some definite advantages over the VHS/VCR format. They offer a cleaner and crisper picture than VHS and you don't have to worry about tracking adjustments or playback "jitters." DVDs also provide a much longer shelf life for videos if they are handled with care. Many of my early VHS videos are no longer viewable or have segments that have deteriorated greatly in quality. I salvaged some by transferring them to DVD format.

One element of DVD recording that can be confusing at first is the various recording formats. These include DVD-R, DVD+R, DVD-RW, DVD+RW, and a DVD-RAM. The secret to understanding these formats is knowledge of two facts:

1. "R" DVDs will only record once, while "RW" Disks can be re-recorded many times; and
2. Your DVD disks must be the same format as the player. So +R disks will not work in –R players. However, for a slight increase in price, you can purchase dual-platform devices that will record and play both formats. The DVD-RAM is an even better quality format but is less common and requires a DVD-RAM player. The multi-format players do not yet support DVD-RAM play.

The bottom line is, if you already own a DVD player and want to purchase a DVD recorder, make sure they have the same format.

Pricing

Many people and schools already have some or all of the necessary equipment to start producing VSM videos. However, let us assume that you are starting from scratch. The basic equipment you need includes: (1) a camcorder, and (2) a VCR and/or DVD/TV combination. Brand name camcorders can be purchased starting at just under $200. As with all equipment, the quality of the product improves with greater price and the best camcorders cost over $1000. Likewise, VCR/DVD combo TVs can begin with 15" to 20" traditional tube TVs for under $200. Even LCD TVs with smaller screens can be purchased for under $350. Thus, $500 can get you started.

If you want to use editing software (as discussed later in the chapter) and already have a PC or Mac, your cost could be limited to the price of the camcorder. Both iMovie© for Mac (Apple) and Windows Movie Maker© for PC (Microsoft) are free from the manufacturers (IMovie comes preinstalled on new computers bundled in a suite of programs called iLife. If you have an older computer that does not have Imovie, it costs $80 to purchase).

A caution for PC users is to make sure you understand the system requirements for using Movie Maker. You may need to install a video card and download or buy software that enables you to burn DVDs. Another problem with Movie Maker is that it will not import video from a DVD. Most PCs come equipped with video cards because they are required for computer gaming. If you need to install a card or replace one that is obsolete, you should probably contact a computer service center. Installing a video card is not complicated, but it is a delicate operation. Macs come ready for video editing and burning. Hopefully, there will either be some fixes to Movie Maker or third-party companies will produce more complete software for video editing. You should do some online investigating of editing software before committing to one if you are PC-based.

Another important consideration is computer memory. Videos consume a good deal of memory. I presently have 7 videos on my computer that range from 2 ½ to 5 minutes in length. The memory used for these videos ranges from 1.7 gigabytes to almost 8. Many computers now come with 160 to 250 gigabyte storage capacity. However, if you plan on storing videos long-term, I recommend obtaining as much memory as possible. External hard drives with 250 gigabytes of memory can be purchased for under $75 and make a very good dedicated storage platform. These attach to your computer via a USB cable and then function identically to your main hard drive. They can be removed when not in use or used to back up the contents of your computer.

There will be other small costs to consider. Camcorders typically require either mini-DVDs or mini-DVD tapes for recording input. The tapes cost approximately $5 to $7, while the mini-DVDs are somewhat cheaper at about $3 each. A tripod is highly recommended unless you have a very steady hand. You can purchase a decent tripod for under $50.

Planning a VSM Shoot When Behavior Is the Concern

Many of the requests I receive for VSM intervention are centered on inappropriate social behaviors, so let's begin by reviewing the steps to take in planning a self-modeling video to change a behavior. Afterwards, I will discuss planning a video to teach a skill.

Step 1: Identify the Behavior to Work On

Identifying the behavior is step one in the planning process. The rule of thumb is that the behavior must be observable and measurable. Anger is not a behavior. A tantrum, on the other hand, is a behavior that can be viewed and measured (in frequency or duration). The following considerations can then be applied in choosing the behavior:

1. The first question I ask parents or teachers who are looking for behavior change is, "Which behavior causes you the most grief or discomfort?" How important is the behavior in the social functioning of the child and/or family? Choose a behavior that causes a great deal of anxiety or stress for participants. Two objective ways to make this selection are to count the number of verbal prompts necessary to get the person to stop (or do) the behavior or to gauge how much of a physical prompt is needed to have the same results. You want the target behavior to be one that significantly affects the child or family.

2. Is the behavior a biological manifestation of the disability? This is a somewhat gray area, but if the behavior is a direct result of the condition (e.g., impulsivity with frontal lobe traumatic brain injury, seizures with epilepsy), it may not be something you can change. The basic tenet of VSM that must be applied here is whether the behavior is within reach or attainable by the person.

3. Is there an appropriate replacement behavior for the one being targeted? When trying to eliminate a negative behavior, the replacement behavior will be featured in the video.

4. How often does the behavior occur? If it occurs very rarely it will be difficult to evaluate results and the filming process will be lengthier. The child may have difficulty "identifying with" rare behaviors. That is, if she only rarely exhibits a behavior, she may not be able to recognize it as part of her actual behavior. For example, a child who has a tantrum every other day will recognize it on screen. The same child may bite, but only rarely and in circumstances that she perceives as very threatening. If you wanted to film a replacement behavior for the biting, the child would be so far removed from the biting that she wouldn't be able to grasp the connection. However, these limitations do not hold true for some academic and language behaviors that the person does not presently use, but that may be very near the person's

ability. Teaching acquisition of new skills via VSM is
quite appropriate. (See the next section.)

If you are choosing a behavior to work on at school, the selected
behavior should be addressed in the child's IEP/IFSP or individual
behavior plan. If you have chosen a behavior to change that is not
in one of these documents, then a meeting should be called and an
amendment added to the plans.

When a behavior is addressed in a child's IEP, the IEP should also
specify how the child's progress is to be assessed. You should include
assessment in your planning process. Chapter 4 goes into assessment
in detail, but suffice it to say here that it is important to have accurate
measures of the rate and/or duration of behaviors prior to and after
intervention with self-modeling.

Step 2: Do a Task Analysis

Some problematic situations such as getting ready for school in
the morning or transitioning between classrooms involve multiple
behaviors. In this case, it is important to break these down into the individual steps or behaviors and to identify which parts of the sequence
are most challenging to the child. These challenging steps can receive
added emphasis in the movie. For example, transitioning between
classrooms might be composed of the following steps:

1. Prompt by teacher or bell that the period has ended.
2. Gather books and supplies necessary for the next class.
3. Walk to the door and stand in line.
4. Teacher says that class may go.
5. Walk from room 111 to 117.
6. Go to desk and get out appropriate materials.

Breaking down a situation or complex behavior into its component parts is called *task analysis*. If you are looking at a sequence of
steps, the child's actual behavior during the steps may be irrelevant
other than it being problematic. Your goal in writing down the steps
is to depict the correct steps in the process.

It would be time prohibitive to treat each problem behavior that
occurs during the sequence as unique and then construct a separate
video for all of them. This would also cause a loss of context and continuity. Instead, it usually makes the most sense to make one video

showing the child using appropriate behavior from start to finish of the sequence. Alternately, you may want to make two videos if two distinct problem behaviors occur during a sequence. For instance, the child may use tantrums and aggression at certain points in her transition from class to class, but also at other times during the school day. In this case, I would look for all the triggers for the tantrums (given that falling to the floor occurs in other situations) and put these scenes in one movie (with replacement behaviors). Likewise, I would identify triggers for aggression and make these the scenes in another movie with the child acting appropriately. But, do keep in mind that VSM often has generalized effects across behaviors, so the first video may lead to changes across behaviors. As you evaluate results, make sure to notice changes in areas other than the one targeted on the video.

Step 3: Identify Replacement Behavior(s)

Once you have pinpointed the behavior(s) you want to change and know when it occurs, you choose a more appropriate behavior to teach the person instead. For example, if a child typically pushes other kids out of the way to be first in line, you might decide to make a visual schedule to show all the class who gets to be line leader that day. You might then teach the child with autism to look at that schedule and see if her picture is on the line leader schedule that day. Or at home, if your child bites her brother when she wants him to give her the TV remote, you might have her tap him on the shoulder or hand him a card with a picture of the remote instead.

The key is to identify a behavior that will enable the person to get her needs met just as quickly and efficiently as the problem behavior does. In some cases, it may help to have an FBA done to help you identify an appropriate replacement behavior.

Step 4: Make a Storyboard

Once you have chosen a behavior or behaviors to teach, you map out what scenes you will film for your video. I do this by sketching out a storyboard.

Task analysis is particularly important in self-modeling because the individual steps can be treated like scenes in a movie. Thus, you can take the six steps involved in transitioning to a new class listed above and include them in a storyboard that is an illustrated representation of the scenes in the movie. As you can see in the illustration of the Dinner Time Storyboard below, you do not need to be an artist to make a storyboard. You can create storyboards using stick figures.

Dinner Time

If possible, have the child participate in this process by helping to define the scenes and creating the drawings that these will represent on the storyboard.

When you are making the storyboard, you can decide whether the video should have a script. Any script can be placed in balloons similar to those in a comic strip.

Scripts can be an important component of self-modeling videos because labeling or naming the behaviors or steps in a sequential process can help the viewer to focus on the important elements. Typically, self-modeling videos begin by labeling the behavior. For example, I have used something similar to the following to lead off the videos I produced: "Here's Alicia! Let's listen to her talking very nicely"; "I don't have to get mad: starring Ian"; "Let's watch Scott eat fast so he can get to play"; "Watch as Jamal talks with his friends and teachers." Putting these statements at the very beginning of the video helps children focus on the salient feature: the behavior you want to target.

Other script elements can be written into balloons in subsequent frames of the storyboard. The script can include actual lines that will be spoken while you are filming the role-playing activity, or it can be lines of a monologue for the child or another narrator that can be inserted before or after a role-playing scene. As an illustration of the latter use of the script, here is how I have used monologue in movies we have done for tantrums: Following a scene in which the child has acted out the appropriate response to a situation that would typically result in a tantrum, we film the child commenting on her own correct behavior (e.g., "If John jumps line, I will ask him to go back. If he doesn't, I will tell the teacher. Getting mad won't help").

Adult narration should be kept to a minimum within the movie. It has been my experience that too many scene cuts to adults and even to peers can serve as a distraction. Remember, the child is the star in this project.

This planning process is somewhat different if you want to eliminate a behavior. First, when focusing on eliminating a behavior, you need to identify what triggers it. (This may require you to do a functional behavior analysis, if you haven't already.) For example, you need to identify events that trigger a child's tantrums or that cause your child to bite her brother or that lead to her flopping on the floor and refusing to move. Each triggering event can then become a scene in the movie and thus be depicted on a storyboard. (The process of observing and recording behavior is addressed in more detail in Chapter 4.)

In this case you certainly don't want to show negative behavior; rather, you want to define a behavior that would be a socially appropriate substitute. To continue the tantrum example, you might decide to show the child being calm when she is not called on in class, asking line jumpers to move back or informing teacher of the transgression, or complying with requests from teachers or parents.

In the particular situation illustrated on the storyboard below, two third-grade students with mild autism were having trouble controlling their tempers in an inclusive class. After a period of observation, four triggers for their tantrums were identified. These included not being called on when they knew an answer, being corrected for errors in academic work (e.g., missing spelling words or math problems on homework or quizzes), other children jumping ahead of them in line, and being asked to clean up before moving to another activity. We then chose a behavior to replace each inappropriate behavior and sketched

Tantrum Storyboard

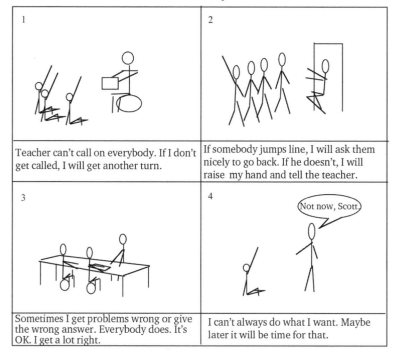

1	2
Teacher can't call on everybody. If I don't get called, I will get another turn.	If somebody jumps line, I will ask them nicely to go back. If he doesn't, I will raise my hand and tell the teacher.
3	4
Sometimes I get problems wrong or give the wrong answer. Everybody does. It's OK. I get a lot right.	I can't always do what I want. Maybe later it will be time for that.

a scene on the storyboard showing the triggering behavior with an appropriate reaction. (Replacement behaviors are best decided on by a team that includes the teacher, the parents, and the child, whenever possible.) For line jumping, we used the classroom rules of first asking the child to move back, and, if this didn't work, politely telling the teacher about the situation.

In this case, the children who would be viewing the videos participated in coming up with the dialogue and discussing alternative ways to react to the situation. If they had not been able to devise their own dialogue, we would have either written simple dialogue (even a single word) that the children were able to say, or we would have had the children communicate nonverbally with the line jumper, such as with a picture symbol. (Interestingly, although the children with autism very much enjoyed role-playing and filming this scenario, the process of filming had no effect on their behavior. However, the day after watching the video, their tantrums miraculously vanished.)

Step 5: Figuring Out How to Get It All on Video

Once you've planned out what you want the video to show, you have to figure out how to get your actor(s) to perform as needed.

This will depend somewhat on the method you will be using to edit the film. You will have a lot more leeway in how you film if you are using video editing software on the computer because your ability to do more intricate editing will be enhanced. Cutting and cropping the video can be done frame by frame, so a missed line or burp can be easily removed. If you are using the VCR method, editing is not so exact. It is much easier if you film until you get the scene right and limit the amount of cutting as much as possible.

The two methods generally used to get children or adults to perform on a VSD video are:

1. role playing, and
2. imitation.

(For an exception, see the section on "Capturing Behaviors When Role-Play and Imitation Are Not Feasible," below.)

Role Playing

This method is appropriate for children who can follow directions and who like to perform—to be "hams." It can be a lot of fun for children when they see the filming as a game. Role playing is the same as acting in a play or class production. More on role playing is found below in the filming section.

Imitation

Some behaviors don't fit well into a role-playing scenario or are more easily obtained through imitation. This is especially true of language production. In the role-playing discussed above, we fed our stars the scripts they were to say. That is basically what is done in imitation: I say (or do) – you say (or do). In this situation, you sit across from the child and the camera is centered directly on her. Usually, all evidence of prompting will be eliminated in the editing process unless the adult or peer prompt is desired in the video (e.g., you are trying to show how to respond to questions). Even if the child is particularly unresponsive, over time you should be able to collect some examples of the behavior you want if you are careful to select a skill that is within the child's abilities.

Imitation can be used across a variety of behaviors. I have used this in every study I conducted in which some form of language production was the targeted behavior. If a child is speaking only in one- or two-word utterances, you can videotape her imitating longer phrases or sentences. Many children within the autism spectrum will readily mimic language spoken by an adult. You just need to know what would come next in the child's language development.

Planning a VSM Shoot to Teach Sequenced Behaviors

As discussed in Chapter 1, VSM has been used to teach a variety of developmental and academic skills in addition to appropriate behavior. Remember, in choosing a skill to teach, you should look for one that is just slightly above the person's current ability level. To do so, it helps to understand the normal sequence of skill development.

Although children develop at different rates, the sequence of skills learned is often much more predictable. Motor development is dependent on the maturation of muscles and nerves that occurs due to a pre-wired DNA code. Unless a physical disability or severe restriction in movement interferes with development, the order of skill acquisition is very predictable. Gross motor development progresses to fine

The author watches Emily as she watches her video on eating a variety of foods.

motor, crawling leads to walking, etc. Much of the way we assess child development is based on these known sequences.

Likewise, new language and cognitive abilities emerge from prerequisite skills. Even children with significant cognitive disabilities tend to follow the same developmental sequence, although often at a slower pace.

We use our knowledge of child development to devise curricula that are appropriate for the ages and abilities of our children, rate toys based on their developmental appropriateness, and base our definitions of developmental delay on how far children lag behind developmental norms. Many of our academic subjects in school also progress along a sequence that gradually moves to more complex and challenging skills. Knowledge of these developmental sequences can also be put to good use in designing self-modeling strategies.

The feedforward concept entails allowing children to view themselves as they could be in the future. We take them one or two steps forward on a known developmental sequence or forward to a social skill we feel is within their capabilities. It might be possible to use self-modeling to train children to do a series of skills along a developmental sequence. A good example of this would be expressive language. For children who are using one-word utterances, you could film them imitating two-word utterances, then three, and so on.

Using VSM to Teach Language Skills

Since most children with autism spectrum disorders are delayed in language skills, let's look in some detail at how to choose a language goal to work on through VSM.

First you need to know what the child's current language abilities are. Then you need to figure out where those abilities fall along the typical developmental sequence.

Here is how you might use your knowledge of the typical sequence of language development to teach more advanced grammar. Say you wanted to teach a child to include the possessive -'s at the end of a noun to indicate what belongs to whom. You would first need to look at how children typically learn morphemes, the smallest units of meaning in a language, including root words, articles, suffixes, and prefixes. (For example, the word "unwashed" is composed of three morphemes: 1) "un-" meaning "not"; 2) wash, the root word; and 3) "-ed" the past tense verb ending.) The prefixes and suffixes that are attached to root words, along with articles, tend to develop in the following sequence:

1. –ing
2. plural –s
3. possessive –'s
4. the, a
5. past tense –ed
6. third person singular –s
7. auxiliary verb be

Carefully note which of these forms the child is presently using and you will be able to tell which morpheme is next in the sequence. If she can already use the –ing verb ending and the plural –s, then she should be ready to learn the possessive ending. That then can become your target behavior. If not, you will need to back up and focus on the previous skills first.

Deciding When to Work on a New Skill

There are two ways you can determine whether a child has mastered a skill sufficiently to move on to the next one in the developmental sequence. First, you could look for emerging language skills, those that the child uses less than 25 percent of the time in *obligated* situations. Here "obligated" means that it would occur in typical, mature language use. Thus, you could be working both on a child's acquisition of a new language skill and her fluency on one that is emerging. This could be an either/or situation based on your perception of the need. If the child seems "stuck" at a fluency level and does not seem to be progressing, it makes sense to concentrate on the emerging behavior. If she makes significant progress in mastering the new language form, then you could move on to the next in the sequence.

Taking already learned skills to a more fluent level fits with Dowrick's definition of "video self-review" rather than "feedforward." The teaching of new skills is "feedforward." Video self-review may be the most logical direction to take with language development because language sequences do not proceed in a lockstep fashion. Typically, children move on to new language skills before they master earlier skills. Thus, they may use one morpheme 75 percent of the time, and the next one in the sequence 25 percent of the time.

Despite the logic presented in the last paragraph, there is some circumstantial evidence that suggests that working on new skills may actually produce better results than working on emerging skills. In this scenario, you would ignore the skills with 75 percent and 25 percent mastery and move on to the next skill in the sequence. This method is somewhat more risky, but also has the potential for better results. The most dramatic results obtained using VSM are achieved when new skills are taught (Dowrick's concept of "feedforward"). Because of the generalization effects attributed to self-modeling, other related skills may improve along with the targeted language skill, including the skill being used correctly only 25 percent of the time. Unfortunately, there is virtually no research that addresses which of these methods is most effective and we must rely on the knowledge of parents, teachers, and therapists to decide on the behaviors to address with any given child.

As stated previously, however, be careful not to try to take the child too far forward in the developmental sequence. Trying to get the child to go from one-word utterances to complex sentences (something you can show on a video with creative editing) is not developmentally appropriate. The upper limit of what you might include in a VSM movie on language is what the child can readily imitate.

Planning a Language Video

To film a language video, it is usually not necessary to develop a storyboard. Storyboards are more useful when making role-playing videos. When you use imitation, a storyboard is typically not necessary because you are focused on one behavior, not a sequence.

If you choose to target a specific morpheme such as "-ing," you would choose root-words that the child presently uses, such as go, jump, run, and have her imitate going, running, and jumping. If you are targeting length of utterance, you would choose words that are relevant (she would understand) and that would be "obligated" if the sentences were more fully developed. For example, "I go" could be expanded to "I go home" or "I go to school." In general, we develop a list of words that we know the child uses and then we add words that are especially relevant and age-appropriate, often dealing with function skills and items the child is likely to want at some point.

When filming a language video, we try to get as much imitation as possible during one sitting so we don't have clothing or background changes. Verbs, nouns, and pronouns are usually our focus with an occasional adjective. With about five verbs and twenty nouns, we can construct many varied sentences. We often try to get the student to say some key prepositions, especially "to." Then we can make relatively long sentences such as "I like to go to school." (See the section on "More Advanced Editing," below, for information on combining words into longer phrases and sentences.)

Using VSM to Teach Academic Skills

There are several areas of academic skill development such as English, math, and reading that lend themselves to filming developmental sequences. English and math are typically taught in a *spiral curriculum.*

A spiral curriculum can be envisioned as looking something like a spiral staircase, with a different skill taught at each step on the staircase. As you move up the staircase, the skills become just slightly more advanced than they were the last time they were taught. They also move through a set sequence so that, for instance, a geometry concept may be followed by a computation skill in addition, which is followed by a measurement skill, which is followed by a multiplication skill, and so on. So, if you were standing somewhere on this staircase and looked straight down over the edge, you would see all the prerequisite skills for the step you are on in a line going to the floor directly below you. If you look above you, you will see the next step in the skill which you will come back to in a few months.

Addition computation would be found on a straight line that bisects all the lines of the spiral. Each time the lines bisect, a slightly more advanced addition skill would be taught. Every skill taught is dependent on prerequisite skills students should have mastered. The sequence of computational skills taught in math has remained the same for several hundred years.

In the third grade, computational skills taught often include the following:

- Adding and subtracting numbers to 10,000 without regrouping
- Adding and subtracting numbers to 10,000 with regrouping
- Subtracting 3-digit numbers with 0's with regrouping
- Memorizing multiplication tables
- Multiplying 1- and 2-digit numbers
- Dividing 1- and 2-digit numbers by one number.

Along with the skills above, you can include simple fraction computation and computation with decimals. Geometry, measurement concepts, and algebra also appear within the spiral curriculum, gradually increasing the complexity of the concepts.

To figure out which academic skill in a sequence a child is ready to learn, it is best to do an assessment. In curriculum-based assessment of math skills, we would present the child a probe (test) with an example of all the computational problems from 1+2 to complex multiplication and division of fractions. We would then look for two things: 1) general achievement level (the demarcation point where everything beyond is too difficult); and 2) holes in the child's learning prerequisite skills that have not been mastered. In short, you would look for skills the child can't do and start working with the earliest in the developmental sequence.

After you choose a skill, the next step is to do a task analysis of the skill. If possible, the movie you make to teach an academic skill should show the child successfully walking through each step in the process. Besides seeing success, the child will illustrate the steps to success. For subtracting with regrouping, the process could be task-analyzed into the following sequence:

1. Start at the top right-hand number.
2. Do "BBB" (bigger-bottom = borrow) check on numbers in the right column.

3. Borrow 10 from the top number to the left if you need to. If you don't, you are free to subtract.

4. Draw a line through the number you borrowed from and make it one less (you can work on teaching the concept of moving 10 later).

5. Move to the next number on the top and do the BBB check.

6. Repeat until you have no more numbers to subtract.

As stated previously, a task-analysis of a behavior can be used as the storyboard; therefore, you would have 6 frames in this storyboard. A finished self-modeling video produced in iMovie or MovieMaker might look like this:

■ **Scene 1.** An opening with a still frame shot of the child working hard at her math. The title would read: "Here's _____ showing us how to subtract big numbers" (add cheers, clapping, etc. as appropriate).

■ **Scene 2.** The child is shown at a seat with a paper of subtraction problems in front of her. She states, "These aren't hard if you know the steps." "First I put my pencil tip on the numbers in the right column." "Next we do BBB." "I look at the two numbers here to see if the bottom number is bigger than the one on top of it." The child moves through the columns until they are all complete and correct and then says, "That wasn't hard. 200 – 123 is 77." Have the child work through another problem or two without the narration until you are sure you have two- to three-minutes of good footage.

■ **Scene 3.** Using another still frame, the child holds up the completed paper, which has a star or some other sign of success that is used in her school. She states, "I did them all right." This is followed by applause and/or children cheering.

Your end product is a movie that should build self-efficacy as well as provide memories of the actual steps in the subtraction process.

There are some important academic skills that don't fit easily into a sequence; yet, often there are ways to depict and film strategies that promote improvement. Take, for example, reading comprehension. This is something that can't be observed other than by evaluating how a child answers questions about the text. Simply filming a student correctly responding to comprehension questions may help boost self-confidence, but the student will not gain skills with which to improve her performance.

For these types of skills, you may be able to use a training model that is similar to a graphic organizer. For example, one common reading comprehension strategy is SQ3R (Survey, Question, Read, Recite, and Review). Students are taught to **survey** the passage by reading the title, subheadings, and the introduction and to look for accompanying graphics or pictures. This is to get a general impression of the subject and to help focus on what the author deems most important. During the next step, **question,** the student turns each of the items surveyed into questions that she thinks will be answered in that section. The idea here is to heighten attention by preparing the student to find answers to predicted questions. Next, the student begins to **read** and fills in the information based on her predictions. After she has read each section, she should stop and determine whether the questions have been answered and whether she can answer all the questions from memory. If not, she must look back at the section until she can **recite** the answers from memory. **Review** is similar to recite, but takes place after the entire passage is read. The student reviews all questions to see whether she can recite the answers from memory. If not, she is to go back over the passage until the questions are answered.

So, while you can't film reading comprehension, you can film the child working on a strategy that will help her comprehension. This would be very similar to a role-playing activity that could be storyboarded. The child would be filmed carrying out each step. In this situation, it would be best to have the student provide a "play-by-play" of what she was doing during each step. For example: "OK, first I look at the title: "The Shadow and the Flash." Now the subheadings: "Two Brilliant Scientists"; "A Clash of Interests…."" You could then film the student formulating questions and following the steps for reading and answering her questions. The finished video would feature the child acting out all 5 steps of the strategy. The storyboard would be dictated by the steps in SQ3R and the content of the reading passage.

Capturing Behaviors When Role-Play and Imitation Are Not Feasible

Some behaviors don't fall neatly on a developmental sequence, nor do they lend themselves to imitation or role-playing. Sometimes a child is not able to imitate or follow directions. Other times, a child with autism may find it too aversive to do a particular activity so there is no way to get her to imitate it.

Using Peers to Show Behaviors

If the child with autism cannot or will not do the target behavior, you may need to produce a video that uses peers as models while incorporating the child with autism in other ways. For example, I have worked with several children on skills related to eating disorders or food aversion. Because of the nature of the problem, it was impossible to catch the rare occurrences when they ate anything outside their usual very limited menu. For these children, we produced videos that illustrated the child in association with food and utensils and used peers as eating models. (Given that we were focusing on **self**-modeling, it was more appropriate to use peers' mouths rather than the total person or face.)

In one case, we made up a game where a four-year-old girl was asked to do the same thing the adult was doing. We picked up utensils, put them in our mouths, used a napkin, etc. This was only partially successful because the child resisted many behaviors related to eating as well as having an aversion to food. We also took footage of the child in the cafeteria and at snack-time. This young girl ate only chicken nuggets, milk, peas, and apples, and the food had to be in the form she was used to (flat chicken didn't work). She would not eat these foods if they were touched by other foods. We captured video of her eating the four foods. Close-ups of other children were taken as they spooned food into their mouths. We zoomed in so that only the mouth and chin were visible (this can only be done well with a camcorder on a tripod, otherwise it will be very difficult to keep the camera steady enough).

We ended up with a series of short video clips representing eating, putting food to the mouth, and using a napkin. We also took videos of the specific cafeteria and snack foods that the parents and teachers wanted the girl to eat. All of these clips were then downloaded to the computer and imported into the editing software. We then sequenced the clips in the order we desired. We recruited some peers as "mouth models" and used some video trickery. We could put the desired food on a fork held by the child and then switch to a close-up of a peer's mouth with the fork and food going in. We also took footage of the desired food and then switched to a shot of the child putting food she did eat into her mouth. We just stood back when filming so the food on the fork wasn't obvious.

Because there was no script associated with these videos, except for the introduction where we labeled the behavior ("Here's Emma eating all kinds of food"), and because the background sound and language were not relevant, we added music. As discussed in the section on "Special Effects" below, this is another easy editing process. In iMovie and Moviemaker, you can click and drag provided music selections or you can import your own music from a music library such as iTunes. On one video, we added soothing ambient music, and on another for a separate student, Beethoven's 9th Symphony. The use of music is something not seen in the research.

When we showed the completed video with the ambient music to the child's teacher, she teared up, even though it was of a child eating. This reaction made me wonder about the potential of music to increase the effect of videos. Certainly, music could at least help maintain the child's interest, as long as it was not overwhelming or distracting. The four-year-old girl who watched the video with Beethoven as the score went from eating four types of food to thirty-three within two months and began asking her parent to try new foods shortly after watching the video for the first time.

Prolonged Videotaping

Cooperating and following directions necessary for role playing and imitation are just not possible for some children. In these situations, you will have to do longer sessions of videotaping to capture rare behaviors. That is, you will need to follow the child around, videotaping her during her daily routine, in hopes that you will see the behavior you are targeting. In some instances, you might be able to set a camera up on a tripod and leave it focused on the child for quite a while (such as while she is sitting in her desk at school).

This can be a long process for certain behaviors. Several of my graduate students once collected about five hours of video for each of three students. We were looking for responses to questions asked by the grad students: there were lots of questions; few responses. In the end, we had two minutes of responses for two of the children and about thirty seconds for the third. These times also included the adult prompt because the children needed to hear the question they were answering. That was enough, and we were able to create videos that made it appear that these children were responding immediately to all questions.

While this method can be particularly laborious and off-putting, there are some scenarios where collecting the necessary footage is not difficult. For example, my colleagues and I have made self-modeling videos this way for several children on the autism spectrum who needed to eat their lunch more quickly. These children had difficulty concentrating on eating during lunch. They gazed around the room, twirled silverware, and found other ways to avoid what one would think would be a pleasant task.

For these children, we set up camcorders to record the half-hour lunch time. Because the children typically remained seated for most of this time, we could just set up the camcorder on a tripod, focus in on the children, and press "record." We did not have to be present until the period was coming to an end. We typically recorded two lunch periods and thus had an hour of tape. Remember that most VSM videos are only two to three minutes long, so we were able to go quickly through the footage and locate scenes where the child put food into his or her mouth. We collected enough of these clips to add up to a couple of minutes, leaving a little time prior to the bite and a little time after. The resulting video made it appear that the child was putting food into her mouth in rapid succession.

Filming

Once you have the completed storyboard and you've powered up the camcorder, you are ready to roll. You become the director and the children, the stars of a movie. If you are using the role-playing method, you can position them, yell "cut," and use other Hollywood jargon. I have been known to don a beret and use a clapper that I got from a game when I call "action." If you are using imitation or capturing rare behavior, the filming proceeds in a more controlled and direct manner.

Just like on a movie set, there are a few checks that you should make prior to shooting. There are some general rules about filming that, if followed, can reduce frustration. These rules relate to:

1. light,
2. camera settings,

3. sound,
4. camera positioning, and
5. getting the footage you need.

Light

Be careful not to film with a strong light source opposite the camera (behind your subjects). It is very frustrating when the filming goes well, but then when you view the video you can only see dark silhouettes against a background of bright windows or sky. If you can't avoid shooting from this position, make sure you limit the amount of bright area in the viewfinder. You may need to lower the camera angle so that more ground or floor is in the shot and less brightness. The child will then appear in the top portion of the video. Make sure you don't lose his or her head in the shot. Cameras automatically adjust for light so you may want to experiment to find the amount of brightness that will cause the foreground to go to silhouette. This will vary from camera to camera.

Camera Settings

In order to keep the video of high quality, there are a couple of things to keep in mind. First, I strongly suggest that you don't use the zoom lens unless absolutely necessary. Digital zoom lenses provide notoriously grainy images. Second, I advise against using the LP (Long Play) mode available on many cameras. You can fit more onto a disc or tape using LP, but the quality is greatly diminished. Children are used to seeing high quality images on their TV screens. Grainy images may be very distracting to them.

Sound

The sound system used on the camera can also affect the quality of the movie. I have two camcorders. One has a good sound system and picks up conversations quite well. The other does not, and I must use a microphone in certain situations. The tiny clip-on lavalier or lapel mikes work very well, especially in a classrooms or school cafeteria, where there will be many voices. In general, we have not found microphones necessary when doing role-playing activities. The children are usually in close proximity to the camera and background noise can be avoided by conducting the session in a quiet area.

Lavalier mikes range in cost from $80 on up. I have found the cheaper models to be sufficient, but do make sure that the model you select will work with your camcorder. There is no universal design in attachments and input devices for cameras.

Positioning the Camera

A tripod is very much recommended, especially when filming children with ASD. Video that has a lot of movement can be distracting and it is quite possible that some children could focus on the "jumpy" nature of the film rather than the images. Using a tripod will provide a steady platform for shooting. A tripod also frees up the cameraperson's hands to a great extent, allowing the director to be more animated and thus more interesting. It also lets the director do physical prompting, if the camera and subject are stationary. If the child is moving, then an extra pair of hands is needed for prompting.

Digital camcorders provide the luxury of a LCD viewfinder so you can see what the picture looks like prior to shooting the scene. You should take advantage of this feature in preparing the scene before you focus on your subject(s). Look through the viewfinder to check for distracting background clutter that should be removed. Ask a peer or adult to stand in the child's place while you get the camera focused in, so you don't use up the child's patience before you begin filming. Then set up the camera as close as you can so you won't distract the child but you won't have to use the zoom.

Getting the Footage You Need

As stated previously, the filming should be enjoyable for all involved. The role-playing aspect of the filming can extend to the adults producing the video as well as the children, as they get to play Stephen Spielberg directing the action. I am amazed at how many children, including very young ones, understand the concepts of "cut," "places everyone," "action," etc.

A typical shooting session might proceed as follows. Conduct a rehearsal. Arrange the children in their places and walk them through the actions depicted in the first frame of the storyboard. If there is any script involved, it can be "fed" to the students immediately before filming. Let us say you want to promote social interactions and the first frame of the storyboard involves having a child with autism ask a peer to go out and play. You can place the peer on the right side of the image in the camera's viewfinder and the target child just outside the visual range of the camera (she will be entering stage left). You just practiced the entrance and the greeting that consisted of a high 5 and the following script: "Hey, Lucius" – "Hey, Johnny" – "Want to go outside and play?" – "Sure, let's go." The director now calls out "Action!" and the stars go through their paces. You may need to go through several "takes" before you get the shot you want. You then repeat this process across all the scenes on the storyboard.

In the preceding example, we assumed that the child can remember strings of words. If the child cannot remember the words, but can read, you can use cue cards—but only as a last resort or if the child is capable of reading fluently and with inflection and emotion. On several occasions we have tried cue cards, but the children read with flat, monotone voices, even though they were good readers. That said, I can see the use of cue cards fitting well into the role-playing activities along with the director, clacker, etc. The child would just need some acting lessons or practice to read like she was talking. All of this would be a good learning activity, over and above making the self-modeling video.

While you are filming, consider whether it would be helpful to turn the LCD viewfinder on the camera to the front so the person being filmed can see herself. (This will only work if the camcorder is within a couple feet of the person and you have a fairly large viewfinder.) Turning the viewfinder around can be a distraction in some cases, but can also give the performer immediate feedback. Some children will "ham it up" a bit when they see themselves and this can be a good thing. I also have used this as a reward, especially if I see any waning in interest.

Whenever possible, you should use the LCD viewfinder to immediately review filmed scenes to determine appropriateness. That way you can avoid having to reassemble everyone to re-shoot a scene that is marred by poor lighting, inaudible lines, etc. More than once I have had to discard video and re-tape entire sessions because of poor quality.

Editing Video

Once you have the raw footage, you are ready to move on to the final step of production. How you proceed from here will depend on whether you intend to use a VCR, a DVD recorder, or a computer with editing software to edit the video.

Editing Tapes Using a VCR

Techniques involved in producing videotapes for VSM are not complicated. In all of my studies and individual applications during the 1990s, I used a camcorder plugged into a VCR for editing. Here are the steps involved:

1. Press the *play* or *fast forward* button on the camcorder and scan the videotape for the appropriate behaviors.
2. Rewind so the tape is at a point just before where the behavior begins, then stop it.
3. Now, simultaneously press the *play* and *pause* buttons on the camcorder. You may need to play and rewind a few times to get this exactly where you want it.
4. You then press *play, record,* and the *pause* buttons on the VCR simultaneously. Both devices are now set.
5. To begin recording the selected video, you just need to release the pause buttons on the camcorder and VCR simultaneously.
6. When the selected video segment is complete, press the pause button on the VCR to stop recording. Using the *pause* button rather than *stop* limits break-up between edited segments and makes for much cleaner transitions.

With a little practice I found that the average time needed to select video segments, edit the tape, and produce a finished self-modeling tape, using this method, is less than one hour, and, depending on the behavior frequency, can be much less.

The "special effects" potential is quite limited using this procedure. You can make and film a sign that labels the child and the behavior. It might read: "Here's Jeffrey talking very nicely," or, "A great reader. Starring Jeffrey Owens." You can also speak the words when you are just beginning to shoot the first scene so that there is an audio

---

Recording with a TV That Has an Auxiliary Channel

Televisions with yellow-red-white inputs also have an auxiliary channel. That is, a channel you need to tune the television to in order to playback or record video. You find the auxiliary channel by turning the TV to channel 3, and pressing the "channel down" button on your remote control or TV until the video playing on the camcorder appears. The auxiliary channel is usually only one or two presses down.

Some TVs that are programmed to cable or satellite won't have the option of pressing the channel down button to find the auxiliary channel. When this is the case, you will need to press the TV/Video button on the remote control until you see your home movie.

When I produce VHS tapes, I use a cheap 15-inch TV/VCR combo that is dedicated to the self-modeling process. I just plug in my camcorder, make sure the TV is set to "Video," and begin my transfer.

---

cue to the behavior. I generally film a sign even if the child does not know how to read because it gives the video one more element that makes it seem like a real TV show and may help the child feel a little more like the "star."

At the end of the tape, you can do something similar in terms of praising the behavior. I tend to congratulate the viewer orally while taping with the lens cover on. This gives you audio over a black background. Having the child pose with a thumbs up while you narrate the praise may work even better. You could also tape children clapping or cheering to add to the end of the tape.

Editing Tapes Using a DVD Recorder

Transferring video from the camcorder to DVD recorder can be as straightforward as transferring video to the VHS format, and you can even use the same kind of audio/visual cable for the transfer. Here are the steps involved:

1. Connect the camcorder to the DVD recorder.
2. Select "pause" and "record" on the recorder.
3. Find the clip you want to transfer on the camcorder by watching the playback on the camera's LCD screen.
4. Press "play" on the camcorder and "pause" on the recorder (to release it).

5. Press "pause" on the recorder after the desired clip is transferred. You then look for the next clip on the camcorder.

A multi-port cable.

There is another option that will transfer the video in higher quality and much more quickly. You can connect a cable known as a *FireWire* (sometimes referred to by PC users as IEEE 1394) from the output port on the camera to the DVD recorder. The camcorder will have several ports that can connect to USB and FireWire ports on the computer or DVD recorder. For someone like myself who has trouble keeping cables organized, you can purchase one connector that has all possible camcorder port configurations on one end and USB and FireWire ports on the other as shown in the photo.

Editing Tapes or DVDs Using Computer Software

Self-modeling tapes created using the VCR method are adequate, although the quality is often less than perfect. Videos made with a DVD recorder/player will be of better image quality than the VCR; however, your range of options for editing will still be limited to cutting and pasting clips onto the DVD.

If you have access to a personal computer, however, the production of high-quality precision videos or DVDs is possible even for the person with modest computer skills. This is thanks in large part to recent developments in computer software, such as iMovie for the Macintosh and Movie Maker for Windows. The editing of videotapes becomes a matter of connecting the camcorder to the computer, downloading the video, and cutting and pasting the selected scenes into a movie. Transitions between video segments and other special effects can be added simply by clicking and dragging the desired item from a menu to the area you want on the video. Transitions such as fade-outs and dissolves greatly enhance the quality of the video. You don't want to overdo the special effects, because they might serve as a distraction, but they can also spice up the video and help hold the viewer's attention.

What follows is a short tutorial on how to use Movie Maker© on the PC. Notes on differences that would be experienced using Apple's iMovie© are noted in the text below.

Once the filming is complete, the next step is to transfer or download the video to the computer and into Movie Maker©. To speed this process and to transport the video in high quality, a FireWire, technically referred to as IEEE-1394 in PC jargon, connection is used. All digital cameras have a FireWire port and many come with a FireWire cable. Unlike the Macintosh, a PC may not come equipped with a FireWire port and the necessary internal card. You may have to have these installed. (If you don't want to invest in a FireWire, you can transfer video more slowly using your camera's USB port.)

One of the main differences between Macintosh computers and PCs is the ease of use of video editing software. The Macintosh comes with everything needed for video editing already packaged and ready to go. PCs typically do not and will probably need additional hardware and software.

Basic Editing

To begin editing, you need to open Movie Maker while your camcorder is on and connected to the computer. You then select "capture from video device" from the "Tasks" menu. You will be asked to name the file, and then a "video setting" page will appear. You should choose the DV-AVI format, which provides the highest quality video. Now you are ready to begin the download. Here you have two options:

1. You can direct Movie Maker to download the entire video from your camcorder, and then you can go off and come back when it is complete.

2. The other option is similar to what you would do in the VCR method by scanning the video using *fast forward* until you come to a desired section of film that you want to download. Then press "capture to download" and "stop" when the desired scene is complete.

A nice feature of editing software is that the controls for the camcorder appear on the screen and you can control all camera functions with a click of the mouse. You should direct Movie Maker to "Create Clips" when you begin your download. This will cause the software to break up your video into smaller clips. The break in the clips is determined by a time stamp from the camcorder or when there is a sudden frame change in the video. Thus, the clips are usually divided just as they were during filming. If you don't click "Create Clips," the video will download everything as one clip. You can break the video into clips later using Movie Maker through a feature called "Detect Clips," but it saves time to do this during the initial download.

You can now start working with the clips that appear in a "tray" to the left of a viewing screen (to the right in iMovie). You can double click on a clip and it will appear in the large screen. You can fast forward to scan quickly through the clip, or you can go even more quickly by clicking and dragging a pointer that appears below the screen. If there is a part of the clip you want to save, you can give it an appropriate title. (They are originally titled "clip 1," "clip 2," etc. when downloaded.) If there is nothing that you feel will make it to the final video, just delete it.

Just below the viewing screen and clip tray there are several horizontal bars. The top one of these is called the "Storyboard." That is where you will drag your keeper video clips. You can do this in any order, and you can change the order any time during the editing process.

After ordering the clips on the Storyboard, switch to the "Timeline" view by selecting "Show Timeline" above the Storyboard. The Storyboard shows only the initial frame from each clip, whereas the Timeline displays both the video and audio components.

Now you can begin the detailed editing process that will allow your creativity to emerge. First, view each clip to see if there is unwanted footage. You can eliminate this footage by allowing the video to play to the point where you want to begin your cut. Then click the "Split Clip" icon in the lower right corner of the Preview screen. (In iMovie, the command "split video clip at playhead" allows you to split clips manually.) This will create two clips from the original one. If these came at the beginning or end of the clip, you can simply delete the undesired clip. If the unwanted footage is in the middle of a clip, you will need to play the clip forward to the end of that footage and split the clip again.

More Advanced Editing

The precision possible with computer software is impressive and allows for some advanced applications. With iMovie, you can move through frames one at a time using the right and left arrow keys. Thus, you can go to a spot on the video and scan left and right until you get the exact spot where you want to cut or paste.

This technique has great potential for teaching language skills. If you have a child who is imitating words, you can precisely cut out each of the words she says and paste them in any order in the video. The editing software typically has a "tray" to hold all of the video clips. Once you have a large enough selection of words (making sure you have some verbs) in the tray, you can start to piece them together into sentences. There is an obvious problem with this method. If you construct a three-word sentence, the child will transform her position in the video three times. Visually it will appear jerky. However, the sentence will sound seamless. Parents have reacted with shock and delight to see and hear their child using sentences. The "jerkiness" in the video does not appear to be too distracting to the children.

Special Effects

Transitions are special effects that allow one clip to flow smoothly into the next. Both iMovie and Movie Maker provide a range of possibilities here. It is recommended that you avoid the more "spectacular" of these transitions and stay with two basic types—dissolve and fade. These are used frequently on TV and in movies, so they shouldn't be distracting to the viewers. You can put a duration on each of these transitions, so experiment to see what looks best. Dissolve involves a morphing between two clips where the first clip blends with the second before the second clip fully appears. This is the most subtle of transitions and is used in our videos more than all the rest combined. The fade involves slowly (although you can also control the timing of this) darkening the end of a clip and then lightening at the beginning of the following clip.

If you have a computer with a microphone, you can do a voiceover either onto the video clips or onto a still frame. In the videos we have used we typically choose a flattering shot of the star that illustrates the target behavior in some way and set this as the opening shot of the video. You can choose a duration for the still frame so that it is slightly longer than the narration. This is where we label the behavior by saying something like, "This is a movie about talking with our friends, starring Renaldo Parsons." You can add sound effects such as children cheering or clapping by clicking and dragging these from a menu. Both Microsoft and Apple have add-on packages with additional sound effects that can be downloaded free. Microsoft has set up a tutorial for Movie Maker that can be accessed at this URL address: www.microsoft.com/windowsxp/using/MovieMaker/getstarted/default.mspx.

As discussed above, we have begun to add music to some video where the language and ambient sound are unnecessary or distracting. Both iMovie and Movie Maker come with a menu of sounds that can simply be clicked and dragged to an area just under the video clips. This area is dedicated to soundtracks. There are sound effects and short musical pieces available on the menus. Both software programs also allow you to choose iTunes as an option for accessing audio. Macs have iTunes built in and recent PCs have followed suit. If this option is available, then your entire iTunes library can be used.

One of the wonderful things about these software programs is that you have complete control of audio. A straight line appears in the center of every clip that represents the audio. Once again, clicking and dragging is all you need to do to lower or increase the volume on any section you choose. To eliminate audio, you just click any point on the line and drag it to the bottom of the clip. If you want to restore volume on a later section, you just go to that section and raise the line. In addition, if you move left or right when you click and drag the line to the bottom, you can fade out the audio slowly or set it to stop abruptly. You can have a lot of fun with this, and, if appropriate, you can have the subject of the video (the star) choose his own score.

The Finished Product

Once a movie is finished, you can make it into a DVD by simply inserting a blank DVD into your computer and clicking "burn." (Macintosh comes with the DVD-making program iDVD already installed.) You can also record the movie directly onto a VHS tape using a VCR. To accomplish this, you export the movie file back to the camcorder, then plug the camcorder into the VCR to record the final tape. This process has been much easier for me when I use a Mac instead of a PC.

Peter Dowrick (1977) has stated that self-modeling tapes need not be longer than two and a half to three minutes to get the desired effects. Longer tapes seem to produce negligible improvements compared to shorter tapes.

Viewing the Video

Once the video is completed, you are ready for the premier. There is nothing set in stone about how best to introduce and show the videos

to children. In school situations, it may be best to allow the student to watch the tape as soon as she enters the building, before classes begin. This eliminates the need to pull her out during important instructional time. It also may be a good idea to arrange a distraction-free setting outside of the classroom. At the Siskin Children's Institute, we have been using the teacher's office that is just off the main classrooms. We set up a portable 19-inch TV-VCR to use for this purpose. Besides the morning viewing, we allow the children to watch the video on demand. You may need to put constraints on some children's viewing, however, if they ask repeatedly. One little boy we videotaped would sign "movie" every time he saw my graduate assistant or myself. Still, if the child shows an interest in viewing the video, it would be fine to allow her to view the video more than once a day.

Interestingly, the time of viewing does not seem to affect outcomes with VSM. You might think it would be most effective to show the video directly prior to an event (for example, showing a video of the child transitioning between classrooms just before the bell rings). However, this does not seem to be the case. Once the child or student watches the video, it seems to have permanence.

In general, adults should limit what they say before, during, or after showing the video. You can make a fuss about the movie "debut" to fit in with the general role-playing idea, and a "good job" at the end is OK. However, do not verbally point out what it is that you want the child to learn from the video. For instance, do not make comments such as "See, you can do that" or "See, you can be nice." This kind of remark can backfire. Remember, one of the strengths of VSM—especially with children with autism—is that no social obligations are present. Do not give the child a reason to erect a defense. Let the child be in control of the video as much as possible.

Caveats and Precautions

However positive the results of VSM studies may appear in the literature, VSM is clearly not a panacea and does not seem to be effective with all students. For example, the staff at the Restructuring for Inclusive Environments Project (RISE) at the University of Memphis used VSM with two children with more severe autism with no positive results. Both of these students were in their mid teens and exhibited significant *perseverative* (ritually repetitive) and self-stimulating behaviors, including hand flapping, pacing, and echolalia. The target behaviors for both students were verbal initiations and responding. Both students were asked to repeat statements read by a RISE staff member, which they did. The students' responses were edited, combined with appropriate questions read by an adult, and then embedded into personal movies. Both students initially watched the tapes with interest, but their attention rarely lasted the entire three-minute duration of the movie. No changes in verbal behaviors were noted in either student. It is possible that the target behaviors were too advanced for the students or that the students did not have the cognitive or attention skills necessary for the intervention.

Certainly, more research needs to be conducted to determine possible limitations of VSM interventions and to find ways to enhance positive effects. Nevertheless, the number of successful applications has far outnumbered the failures.

Video self-modeling is, by definition, a very positive method. Still, there are both methodological and ethical precautions that should be taken. When applying VSM, it is extremely important to select developmentally appropriate behaviors. One of the only ways in which self-modeling could have a negative result is by providing children with images of themselves doing things that are far beyond their ability to master.

If professionals other than parents are using VSM with a child, it is important to obtain *informed consent* from the parents. Informed consent means that parents have a thorough understanding of what the method entails so that their agreement to use VSM goes well beyond a simple signature. A related consideration is that parents should know exactly what will happen to any of the videos used with their child and must agree to how these are used in the future. In our research we provide three options to parents and caregivers:

1. All copies of the videos are destroyed at the end of the study.
2. They receive a copy of the video and all others are destroyed.
3. We keep a copy to be used for educational purposes (at conferences and in college methods courses) and they receive a copy.

The confidentiality of students with disabilities is also protected under the Individuals with Disabilities Education Improvement Act (IDEA) and the Family Educational Rights and Privacy Act (FERPA). Any dissemination of personally identifiable information in any format is strictly forbidden unless parent consent has been obtained. The bottom line is that every precaution possible should be taken to ensure confidentiality while at the same time making sure that everyone understands what is occurring.

One of the issues that falls into a gray area is whether an amendment to the IEP is necessary when VSM is used in classrooms. VSM could be considered just another method used by the teacher to reach the objectives listed on the IEP, thus requiring no changes. However, it is best to err on the side of caution. The senior staff of Siskin Children's Institute debated this question and finally decided that self-modeling was "different" enough to constitute a change in programming. Accordingly, we combine a meeting with parents to discuss an amendment to the IEP, provide them the information about VSM, and request that they sign the Informed Consent form. A sample Informed Consent form is provided at the end of this chapter.

How to Incorporate VSM into a Student's IEP

Rarely are specific teaching methods addressed in the IEP unless they are out of the ordinary. At this point in time, VSM might be considered extra-ordinary and as such should be addressed in the IEP. Certainly the filming itself, along with the releases needed and confidentiality issues, warrants special attention.

IEP goals and objectives typically have three components:

a. conditions under which the behavior will occur;

b. the behavior or skill targeted; and

c. criteria(on) for success.

In behavioral objectives, these three components often lead off with the following words/phrases respectively: a) given...; b) the child will...; c) with.... When writing goals and objectives for the IEPs or lesson plans, VSM will most likely appear in the conditions—for example, "Given a 3-minute video of Sarah successfully using "to be" verbs in sentences, she will...."

Many long-term goals are written more generically, often omitting "conditions" and expressing criteria in general terms—for example, "Raoul will learn to add two-digit numbers with renaming," or "Rhonda will improve her skill in oral expression." Simply adding something like "via VSM" to the end of these goals should suffice to meet any compliance issues and serve as a segue to discussion of the method.

Many IEPs will contain a question such as the following to address adaptations needed for general education involvement: "What type(s) of adapted instruction is necessary for the student to make effective progress?" This is another area of the IEP where VSM could be addressed.

It might be time-efficient to deal with the releases and explanation of VSM (as part of informed consent) at the time of the IEP meeting. If an IEP is already in place, an amendment will need to be added.

The following are examples of goals and objectives that involve VSM:

- Given a self-modeling video of the steps involved in successfully completing addition problems with regrouping, Roger will successfully complete these types of problems during assessments with 90% accuracy.
- Using VSM to supplement her other language instruction methods, Vera will increase her mean length of utterance to 4.

- Through the use of VSM and simulation activities, Shaquille will successfully participate in job interviews.

VSM Do's and Don'ts

DO
1. Depict only positive behaviors.
2. Select behaviors that are developmentally appropriate.
3. Keep the video under 5 minutes.
4. Ensure confidentiality if the video will be used by schools or agencies.
5. Make sure there is an IEP or IFSP link.
6. Get **informed** consent from parents/caregivers.
7. Make the filming process fun.
8. Include the child in planning, if possible.
9. Learn new technology skills.
10. Allow the child to view the video daily and when requested, if possible.
11. Allow the child to watch the video without adult comment if the video includes a clear written or verbal statement about the featured behavior.

DON'T
1. Depict negative behaviors.
2. Select behaviors that are too advanced.
3. Get carried away with the editing (use too many special effects).
4. Force the child to view the video.
5. Begin without parental informed consent.
6. Expect miracles.

Parental Consent Form

As part of an effort to determine the effectiveness of video self-modeling (VSM) on the _____ skills of children with pervasive developmental delay or who are on the autism spectrum, I would like to try this method with_____ _____. This research will in no way affect the material or instruction your child presently receives. It is a project designed to determine whether children watching themselves _____ will _____.

VSM involves "staging" interactions and catching them on video. We do this in two ways: 1) We take video of a child imitating or role playing the behavior in a positive way; or 2) We film the child hoping to catch rare behaviors. Then, using video editing software, we take the best footage and combine it into a short video—no more than 3.5 minutes. We then allow the child to watch the video in the morning prior to instructional time.

Your child's privacy will be protected at all times. Your child's anonymity will be of utmost importance to us and we will be diligent in our efforts at confidentiality. There will be no adverse consequences for your child. In the best case scenario, your child will improve _____. The worst-case scenario is that we will see no change in_____, but you will have a nice video of your child.

We will observe your child for any changes in behavior following watching the video and will communicate to you if we do see changes. We would also like to hear from you if you see changes at home.

The videos produced will only be viewed by the classroom professionals and your child. At the conclusion of the project, you will determine the fate of the videos. We can destroy all video footage, we can destroy what we have and provide you with a DVD of the video, or you can allow us to use the video for educational purposes (for presentation to education students and at conferences where we may be presenting). At the conclusion of the study, we will share results with you, and, if you wish, we will train you in video self-modeling techniques.

Participation in this project is voluntary and there will be no adverse consequences should you not wish your child to participate. If you do agree to your child's participation, that permission may be withdrawn at any time by contacting _____.

_____   _____
(signed)   (date)

I,_____, *give permission for my child*_____
(Parent/Guardian's Signature)   (Child's Name)
to participate in the research project.

3 | Evaluating Your Results

How can you tell if your child or student has improved, and, when improvement is obvious, how much progress has been made? It only takes a little knowledge and effort for you to measure the gains—or lack thereof.

Sometimes our perceptions can be deceptive. When we want to see gains, we develop a natural bias that can cloud our objectivity. We may notice things that escaped our attention before simply because we are more focused on a particular behavior, or we may be so optimistic about a new technique that we misinterpret what we see. Researchers go to great lengths to control these types of variables to keep them from influencing their work. We always build in an inter-observer agreement element to our studies by having at least two observers evaluating the same child at the same time and then comparing results. If we do not have high agreement, then our findings lack reliability and are rendered meaningless.

When we use techniques at home or in school we do not need to establish tight controls like these. We do, however, want to know how effective an intervention is. To do this, we need objective measures of the behaviors prior to and following intervention. We often refer to the behavior prior to intervention as *baseline*. Baseline measures can be:

- the number (simple tallies) of the behavior we are trying to change—for example, the number of times a child pushes peers or the number of times a child puts a spoon to his mouth during lunch.

- the rate (occurrences per minute) of the behavior—for example, while watching a child eat for 3 minutes, he put the spoon to his mouth 9 times. His rate would be 9 ÷ 3 minutes = 3 occurrences per minute.
- the duration (length of time) of the behaviors—for example, your child rocks back and forth while sitting on the floor. The first time he does this in the day, his rocking lasts for 1 minute, 30 seconds. The second time, it lasts for 2 minutes, 2 seconds. You can compute an average; in this case, it is 1 minute, 46 seconds.

The behavior itself must be one that is easily observed so that measurement can be objective. You also do not want to measure vague or global behaviors like times a child became angry or upset. You need to be more specific. Instead of trying to assess anger, you can measure times a child throws objects, the duration of tantrums, or the rate of verbal outbursts. A simple rule of thumb is that you must be able to see or hear a behavior in order to take data on it. You may also want to start with a behavior that occurs rather frequently so that you have more data to evaluate.

Collecting Data

There are several ways one can collect data, including keeping a tally, and measuring durations. Which method you use to collect data is somewhat dependent on the behavior.

Keeping a Tally

Keeping a simple tally of occurrences is appropriate when the behavior occurs often enough that you can't remember every instance or you have other duties that prohibit constant surveillance or keep you at a distance from the child. You can jot down tallies on paper or you can purchase a cheap handheld counter (available online or at sporting goods stores for under $10) that will give you more freedom of movement. You can keep the hand counter in a pocket and manipulate it there so the child doesn't realize he is being observed. (If a child knows he is being observed, it can affect his behavior.) Some people put masking tape on the back of their wrist and make tally marks on it to record behavior frequencies.

Measuring the Duration of a Behavior

Measuring the duration of events can often provide you with more information than you can get from just recording occurrences. If you wanted data about tantrums, you could record either number of tantrums or the duration. For example, you might note 2 tantrums on Monday and 1 on Tuesday, giving you data points of 2 and 1, if you went with number of occurrences. This gives you a baseline rate of 1.5 tantrums per day. In contrast, your scores for duration might be 16 and 9 minutes, with an average tantrum length of 12.5 minutes. There would be little room for improvement if your baseline rate of tantrums was 1.5. You would be much more likely to see changes using the duration measures in minutes. This will also allow you to detect smaller degrees of change.

You can also use this method to measure positive behavior. For instance, you might use the method if you are trying to increase the time a student stays on task or sits in his chair without running around.

If you are measuring the duration of a behavior, it is a good idea to have a stopwatch that you can click at the start and end of each event. You can then record the length of time for each tantrum or other behavior and at the end of the day total up the times. Place that total on the graph.

How Often to Collect Data

A good way to organize your data collection is through *interval recording*. This is when you divide observation periods into smaller, equal time periods (e.g., 10 minute intervals). You can make your observations at random times throughout the day or during the time of day when the behavior is known to occur. You can either mark whether or not the behavior occurred during each interval or you can mark the total number of occurrences.

A related method of recording data is *time-sampling.* Here you record data periodically over identical lengths of time. A major advantage of this method is that the observer does not have to focus on the behavior for long periods. Three fifteen-minute periods a day could be sufficient. Again, you could either record whether the behavior occurred during the period or you could keep a running tally. The latter method would give you a better indicator of the rate of the behavior. You would then transfer the data to a graph using either observations or dates as the x-axis (horizontal line of the graph). If you used the method of only recording whether or not a behavior occurred during an observation session, you will probably need to use days of observation; otherwise, you will only have scores of 0 and 1. See the sample graph in Figure 3-1.

Another method for collecting data is to *obligate* the use of a behavior. Here obligate is defined as setting up a situation so that the behavior you want to see would typically occur, or be obligated, in normal circumstances. Good examples of obligated behaviors are responses to requests and questions. A request obligates an action and a question obligates a communicated response. Thus, if you wanted to measure the child's response rate to questions, you could either ask a set number of questions and record the number of responses (e.g., 2/10) or you could ask varying numbers of questions and record the percentage of responses (e.g., 2/10 = 20%, 3/18 = 17%...).

Setting Up the Design

Back in Chapter 1, an overview of single-subject design was presented. In its simplest form, a single-subject design will have two phases: baseline (pre-intervention) and intervention. A third phase is often adopted for use at the end of a study so that you can measure the very important concept of *maintenance,* which is the staying-power of a treatment: During this phase, you withdraw the intervention so you can see how effective it is over time once it is stopped.

The visual depiction of data is a central element of single-subject design. Recording data points on a graph will allow you to determine whether change is occurring and whether that change is directly related to the intervention.

It is easy to record data on graph paper. A column on the left side of the paper will have a measure of the skill or behavior that you are focusing on. You can estimate the range you will need to have in the column after a few observations. Let's say you are measuring the duration of tantrums. On day one, your child had two tantrums that lasted 8 minutes each for a total of 16 minutes. On day two, he had a tantrum that lasted 9 minutes. Based on the totals of the first two days, a scale

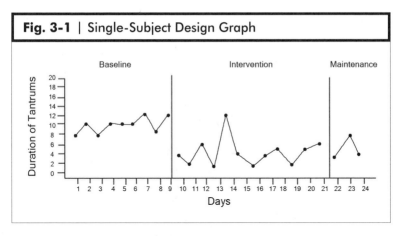

Fig. 3-1 | Single-Subject Design Graph

ranging from 0 to 20 minutes with intervals of one or two minutes seems appropriate. Make sure that the intervals are equally spaced.

The bottom of the graph typically has a measure of time or numbered observations. The bottom line could be labeled either day 1, day 2, etc. or observation 1, observation 2, and so on. Once you have both sides of the graph labeled, it is just a matter of placing a dot above the appropriate time and directly across from the measure of the behavior. The set-up for a single-subject design graph is shown in Figure 3-1.

Did It Work?

One of the nice features of single-subject designs is that you can analyze your results simply by inspecting your graph. Ideally you would want to see a stable (flat) baseline phase followed by a change, represented by a spike on the graph, shortly following intervention. You might even see a change during the baseline phase at the point where you did the filming for the video—especially if you used the role-playing method. Filming in itself can be a powerful intervention. If your child's or student's behavior does change right after you do the filming, you may want to wait until the baseline rate stabilizes again before trying the self-modeling videos.

Somewhat surprisingly, changes occurring following role play are rarely noted in the research. Acting out positive behaviors would seem like a good intervention in itself, but maybe the short length of time involved with this activity inhibits a noticeable change. The bot-

tom line for parents and teachers is that they want to see a change in the student's behavior or ability following instruction or interventions. You may wonder why it matters whether the change was caused by role playing or by watching self-modeling videos. In fact, it is important to pinpoint what actually caused change because knowing the strength of a method gives us knowledge that we can apply in the future and to other skills.

Although it is possible, do not expect to see slow, continuous growth on the graph. You should instead see a substantial spike on the graph following intervention. If you do not, the chances are small that gains will start after your child has viewed the video over time. I know of no cases where there has been a lag between intervention and observable results. The only times that a child's behaviors changed after a period of time had passed following the initial viewing were when the original video was significantly altered and shown in a new format. Thus, a general rule for evaluating results is that if the person's behavior does not change soon after watching the video, you probably will not see change later on.

Another attractive feature of using graphs to evaluate your results is that the degree of change is easily quantifiable. For example, you will be able to be specific in stating the change in duration of tantrums simply by referring to the graph (1 hour and 12 minutes on day 3 versus 5 minutes on day 8).

In cases where the baseline and intervention phases are relatively unstable, with peaks and valleys appearing on the graph, you can compute averages for each phase for comparison purposes. Averaging may also help if the differences between intervention and baseline are more subtle.

While change typically occurs immediately after intervention with VSM, the degree of change is variable. This raises what is probably the most important question in evaluating the effectiveness of any intervention: What degree of change is significant? Another way of describing this is "do the ends justify the means?" Are the results obtained positive enough to justify the expenditure of time and effort expended to achieve those gains? The answer to that question can only be provided by those intimately involved in the child's instruction. Having quantifiable measures of children's gains will provide parents and educators with more exacting information that they can use to make those decisions.

Joining the Community of Researchers— The Siskin Children's Institute Center for Self-Modeling Studies

If you were able to make it through the review of research presented in Chapter 1, you know that the scope of our knowledge of VSM is relatively limited and there are questions that have yet to be answered about age of effectiveness, range of behaviors, types of disabilities, and optimal contents of the videos.

I had two main purposes for writing this book. The first was to disseminate information about a technique that I feel has great promise for those who work directly with children with autism and other developmental disabilities. My second motive is more scientific in nature. I want to add to our knowledge base of VSM and to provide the opportunity for parents and educators to be part of that process.

Anecdotal reports are often dismissed by the scientific community for understandable reasons. These typically lack the controls and objectivity necessary to make definitive statements about a treatment approach. However, researchers place much more weight on single reports of results if some degree of control has been practiced and the results have been quantified. Add to this the potential for many parents, teachers, and others to report the results of their VSM treatments, and to apply VSM to new areas and you have a format for expanding our knowledge base. This is what we are trying to accomplish with this book and the companion website at the Center for Self-Modeling Studies: www.siskinvsm.org.

We invite you to submit your findings, whether positive or not, to this website, and to share anecdotes about your experiences with

VSM. Part of the website will be a clearinghouse for reports from parents and educators about their experiences and results. It would be wonderful to receive graphs and data showing results of VSM usage that could go into a database, but written anecdotal accounts will also be very welcome. If you decide to submit something to the site, be assured that anonymity will be strictly enforced. It is probably best to use pseudonyms if you feel the least bit uncomfortable about sharing information.

Families may also submit their videos with whatever restrictions they desire on how they are used. It would be helpful if families state restrictions on how they want the information they submit to be used. The following checklist gives several options:

- ☐ 1. Information may go into the Center database, but is not to be shared or published in any way.
- ☐ 2. Information can be used for educational purposes, including use in college courses and conference presentations.
- ☐ 3. Quotations can be extracted from case studies and used on the website and for presentation at conferences and college courses.
- ☐ 4. Staff may use written information for educational purposes, but may not disseminate videos in any way.
- ☐ 5. Videos can be used on the website and for educational purposes.

Please note: Professionals who work with children should not contribute videos, because there are too many confidentiality issues even if parent permission is obtained. Feel free to encourage parents to contribute videos, however.

Another section of the website will focus on technical assistance for those who want to start using VSM or who have troubleshooting questions during the process. Someone from the Center for Self-Modeling Studies at the Siskin Children's Institute will be available to provide technical assistance every day during the work week. The site will also contain a forum for ongoing discussions among parents and professionals about their children and methods used to educate them. Additionally, a blog will be available so that people can track the day-to-day activities in our research center and school. I believe that this companion website is unique, and, like self-modeling, has great potential. I strongly urge you to visit it, communicate with us, and become partners in the growing knowledge base of video self-modeling.

4 | Real-Life Applications of Self-Modeling

This chapter presents actual case studies illustrating the process of using video self-modeling, from identifying behaviors to analyzing results. The treatments were carried out in partnership with staff either from the RISE Project in Memphis, Tennessee (Restructuring for Inclusive Education) or the Siskin Children's Institute's Early Learning Research Center in Chattanooga, Tennessee. Some of the cases described were part of published studies, while others involved individuals who were referred to me by teachers or parents. All were carried out in controlled conditions such as those described in the last chapter. Even though we could have been less formal in our data collection and methods, we wanted to be relatively sure that it was the VSM causing any changes rather than some other variable.

For the most part, I have selected examples of our work that had the most remarkable results. You are not supposed to use the word "remarkable" when describing results of studies, but you will see that in some cases the results were…remarkable. Also keep in mind that in many of these cases, a variety of other methods and strategies had been previously tried to shape or extinguish behavior, but to no avail.

Case Study 1—Ivan: Getting Ready for School
(Using VSM Role-Playing to Change Behavior)

Ivan, age 10, had been diagnosed with Asperger's syndrome and oppositional-defiant disorder. He was a Russian orphan who had been adopted and brought to the United States when he was 5. Ivan's problems were more of an issue at home than at school, so the intervention was carried out at his home. His parents were asked to identify the behavior that caused them the most frustration. This turned out to be getting him ready for school. Prior to intervention, the parents were asked to time Ivan and to record the number of prompts they used during that time period. Over a three-day period, Ivan took an average of 60 minutes from wake-up to getting ready to go out the door, and his parents averaged about 10 prompts that mainly involved telling him to hurry up. They reported that this was typical.

The parents were asked to tell Ivan and his younger sister that someone was coming to make some movies with them. Then, when I first arrived, I made movies of the children posing and doing several fun activities of their choosing. The children were allowed to immediately view the videos as they were played back in the camcorder. This was designed to break the ice and get Ivan accustomed to the camera and my presence.

Next, the parents, children, and I sat down at the kitchen table to plan the video and determine which scenes to film from Ivan's morning routine. We did a task analysis of the time from waking to leaving the house and then arranged in scenes on a storyboard. The storyboard was a plain sheet of paper divided into 6 rectangles. Each rectangle represented a scene, and stick figures and crude representations of the environment were drawn for each scene. Ivan's storyboard is shown on the next page.

The filming proceeded almost flawlessly. Ivan enjoyed the role playing and cooperated and performed extremely well. It was a Sunday afternoon, but he gladly changed into his pajamas for the first few scenes. Prior to filming each scene, we went over the script and sometimes did a brief rehearsal. We discussed the dressing and bathroom scenes and we came up with solutions that Ivan felt comfortable with. (For example, getting dressed was illustrated by him pulling on his shirt. Going to the bathroom was walking toward the bathroom, stating where he was going, and then walking in and closing the door.)

I edited the raw footage at Ivan's house using the camcorder–VCR method. Due to the role-playing format of the video, there was no parental prompting except for the initial "wake up" call. Had there been any prompting, however, we would have eliminated it during the editing process. We only had to remove one scene that the mother

Getting Ready for School

Scene 1 - bedroom	Scene 2 - bathroom
1. Wake up 2. Make bed	3. "Time to go to the bathroom." 4. "I have to get dressed now."

Scene 3 - bedroom	Scene 4 - kitchen
5. Dressing = Pull shirt down 6. Go downstairs	7. Eat breakfast 8. Feed dog 9. Back upstairs

Scene 5 - bathroom	Scene 6 - kitchen
10. Brush teeth 11. Back downstairs	13. Hugs goodbye 12. Get coat and backpack 14. Out to bus

Ivan's Storyboard

did not like and one scene in which Ivan went into the garage for dog food and was gone for some time. We had about 5 minutes of footage total. It only took a few minutes of scanning the raw footage to locate the two clips we wanted to cut and then eliminate them by turning off the record button on the VCR when they came up. A brief recording of my voice stating the behavior ("Let's watch Ivan get ready for school") was added to the beginning by simply covering over the lens and using audio only. We ended up with a three-and-a-half-minute tape.

I instructed Ivan's parents to let him watch the tape whenever he wanted and to refrain from urging him to watch it. I also asked them not to compare his actual behavior to his behavior on the tape. Finally, I asked them to continue timing his *getting ready* behavior and recording the number of prompts.

Ivan watched the tape once just after completion and once that evening before bed. The next day, I was awakened by a call from Ivan's father, who asked, "OK, now what do we do for the remaining 40 minutes?" Ivan had completed his normal morning routine in slightly over 20 minutes. The only prompt his parents had to give him was to wake up. Ivan maintained this rate of getting ready for school over an extended period. Four months later, Ivan's parents called me for a copy of the master tape. They had taped over their copy and they said Ivan had regressed somewhat. It is unclear how effective this "booster shot" was because the family relocated soon after.

Case Study 2—Jeremy: Responding to Questions
(Using Extended Videotaping When Role Playing Is Not Feasible)

For students with more severe autism, the role-playing method may not be appropriate. Taping the child until he or she demonstrates the behavior enough times to make a two- to three-minute tape may be necessary. Of course, this requires the student to have a baseline rate of behavior. That is, he or she must demonstrate the behavior at least occasionally in order to capture it on film. This method of creating a self-modeling video can often be time consuming.

Several graduate assistants and I (Buggey, Toombs, Gardner, & Cervetti, 1998) used this method to increase the verbal responses of three middle school students described as having moderate to severe autism. We conducted play sessions in their homes, where we asked them frequent questions. Most of the questions required only one-word responses and mostly required naming objects (e.g., Who is this?, What is this?, What color is it?). During the initial play sessions and taping, responses were rare. They did occur, though. For the most "responsive" student, Jeremy, we were able to amass two minutes of questions and responses from almost six hours of raw footage. The responses were taken from this footage and edited into a 2-minute 30-second video. Several of his clearest responses were repeated more than once on the tape. One of the students had only three responses in six hours. These three responses were looped continuously to produce a two-minute tape.

After watching their completed VSM videos, all three students made good gains in their rate of responses. Jeremy made extremely impressive gains. In subsequent play sessions with Jeremy, we allowed him to view the video before beginning the normal activities carried out in previous sessions. For our data collection, we used percent of responses to questions. Jeremy's progress is shown on the graph in Figure 4-1. Jeremy more than doubled his rate of responding in general, and responded 100 percent of the time to some specific questions such as "What color is this?" and "How many _____ are there?"

The major drawback of the method we used with Jeremy was the time investment. The results in this case justified the time, but the feasibility of investing this much time for individual behaviors when the outcome is not certain might be questionable. When a teacher has larger numbers of children in the classroom, using this method might be even more problematic. Still, it might be appropriate to use this method with the most significant behaviors. In addition, parents might be willing to put in the time filming their children if it might help their

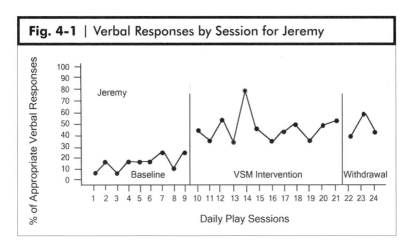

Fig. 4-1 | Verbal Responses by Session for Jeremy

children improve their behavior or skills at home or at school. After all, the Lovaas method of Applied Behavior Analysis requires 40 hours of therapy per week.

Case Study 3—Ronnie, Eating Lunch
(Gathering Raw Footage When Role Playing Is Not Feasible)

Sometimes a child is not able to role play, but it is relatively simple to capture his or her behavior on film and then edit out the footage that is not relevant to the self-modeling video. In these cases, gathering raw footage is not nearly as intense as it was for Jeremy. This method was used with Ronnie, an 8-year-old child with moderate autism who never finished his lunch.

The RISE staff began working on a self-modeling video for Ronnie in early November. At that time, Ronnie had not had any free-play time, which was only allowed when students completed eating and cleaning up before lunch was over. Ronnie was very distractible and needed frequent prompts to attend to his lunch. He was often observed mumbling to himself, laughing aloud for no apparent reason, and self-stimulating by twirling his silverware.

A camera with a tripod was placed in the lunch room and focused on Ronnie. Two 30-minute lunch periods were taped. One of the RISE staff took the raw footage home and transferred it directly into his computer. Using iMovie on a Macintosh computer, it was relatively easy for him to cut and paste every instance of Ronnie putting his spoon to his mouth and chewing. The footage that didn't show Ronnie eating was highlighted much like in a word processing program and deleted, leaving a clip of exactly what we wanted in the final video. The process was not very time-consuming, either. Using fast-forward, the 60 minutes of tape were analyzed in 20 minutes.

The staff member then chose a flattering shot of Ronnie, created a still frame, and placed it at the beginning of the movie. On this frame, both voice and written attention was given to the behavior ("Ronnie's movie! Here's Ronnie eating at lunchtime!") Crowd cheering was added by clicking and dragging it from a menu of sound effects. Lastly, using the click-and-drag method, transitions were added between each scene (behavior), giving the movie a look and feel of a professional video.

Ronnie's response to the video was one of the most dramatic we have seen using this method. He watched the film the first day after it was completed on a Thursday afternoon. He was absent Friday and Monday and returned to school late in the morning on Tuesday. Thus, he had not had the opportunity to watch the tape since the initial viewing. This first day back, Ronnie finished his lunch with minimal prompting, cleaned up his space, and had a few minutes of free time. Ronnie watched his tape over the next week and his self-stimulating behavior virtually ceased and he consistently finished his lunch and had free time. Ronnie maintained this behavior throughout the school year. Even on days when he did not finish his lunch, he said he was done, cleaned up, and was able to have some free time.

The results depicted in Figure 4-2 show the dramatic change Ronnie experienced. Because his lunch was packed in the same Tupperware container every day, it was easy and convenient to use percent of food eaten to measure his progress.

Ivan and Ronnie both made dramatic progress through VSM. Both had been on intensive ABA regimens targeting the behaviors in question with little or no success. These rapid changes in behavior after implementing VSM were not expected. While we had seen significant gains across an array of behaviors for other children with various degrees of autism, few were as dramatic as these two cases. Nevertheless, we have found VSM to be very effective with many students with autism spectrum disorders. We have seen the duration and number of tantrums decrease rapidly, social initiations and language usage increase (Buggey, 2005), and many negative behaviors during classroom transitions decrease.

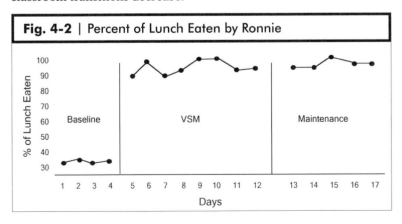

Fig. 4-2 | Percent of Lunch Eaten by Ronnie

Case Study 4—Scott and Aaron, Tantrums
(Using Scripted Role Play to Change Behavior)

Our work with children and their tantrum behaviors may have provided some insight into how the VSM process works. Two children with Asperger's syndrome, 7 and 8 years old, exhibited very similar behaviors leading up to and during tantrums. They both would frown and fold their arms across their chests. Their shoulders would rise into a defensive position so that their necks were almost not visible, and then they would either go limp and fall to the floor or start crying hysterically. The behaviors were probably so similar because they had been in the same room together for over a year.

In preparation for trying VSM to reduce Scott and Aaron's tantrums, a functional behavior assessment was conducted to determine what caused or triggered the tantrums. The triggers for the students varied somewhat, but there were commonalities as well. The major triggers were: being corrected on academic work, not being called on when they knew an answer, students jumping in line ahead of them, and having their requests refused. These four triggers became the four frames of the storyboard, as shown in the storyboard on page 49.

Using the storyboard as a guide, the teachers set up situations that normally triggered tantrums, using classmates acting as co-stars. Scott and Aaron were instructed in appropriate responses and these were scripted and rehearsed for the performance. We then made a personal video for each boy. During the filming process, both performed well, although occasionally one or the other started the pre-tantrum aura before being reminded that he was in a movie.

The videos began with both students labeling the behavior: "When things don't go right, I am going to stay cool." This was followed by the usual cheers and clapping. We then moved into the individual scenes. Each scene was followed by the student offering himself some positive reinforcement—for example, by stating, "Wow, I handled that really well!"; "I know Ms. _____ will call on me soon"; or "Hey, that worked really well!" At the end of the tape, the students themselves commented on how grown up they had behaved. Because these two boys had so much fun with the VSM process, we added some out-takes at the end. One of them showed Aaron starting to tantrum before being reminded we were just acting. He laughed and gently smacked his forehead with his palm.

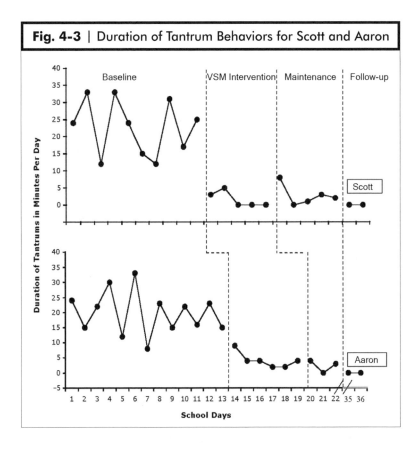

Fig. 4-3 | Duration of Tantrum Behaviors for Scott and Aaron

The videos were easy to edit, as many of the scenes went as planned, and those with problems were immediately re-shot following a cry of "cut!" from the "director." We waited a few days before showing Scott and Aaron the final video to make sure that their role playing did not affect their baseline tantrum rate. Both children's behavior changed dramatically after the first viewing of the video. Almost immediately, the number of tantrums and their durations decreased markedly. A single subject design was used to evaluate results and is presented in Figure 4-3.

Because we had two students working on the same behavior, we set up a multiple-baseline design. This allowed us to start the intervention with Scott while we continued to collect baseline data on Aaron. In other words, Scott got to start watching his video before Aaron got to watch his. Both of these children radically changed behaviors in what one of the teachers referred to as a life-changing event. In addition, the students were observed for another six months and showed no regression to tantrum behaviors.

What impressed the teachers most was what sometimes happened shortly after Scott and Aaron began their typical pre-tantrum behavior. On several occasions, the students made comments like "whoops," "forgot," or "darn"; ceased the behavior; and returned to what they had been doing. It seemed as if they were referring to the memory of the tape. Both students exhibited this type of self-correcting behavior.

If it is so easy for people with autism and other developmental disabilities to replay these memories, it might explain the generalization effects so often reported in the VSM literature. The students carry the memories wherever they go and might not need other environmental reminders or prompts to trigger a response. Scott and Aaron both seemed to overcome conditioned responses to environmental triggers. According to their parents, they also generalized their new anger management skills to other conditions not included in the videos, including their homes.

Case Studies 5 & 6—Ryan & Alan, Expressive Language
(Using Frame-by-Frame Editing)

The precision that can be attained with editing software has led to new uses for video self-modeling that were never possible with the VCR/camcorder method. Using the left and right arrows keys on the computer to move between individual frames, you can now edit frame-by-frame. We have taken advantage of this feature in our work with children with language delays. For example, we have cut individual words spoken by the students and pasted them into sentences. We have used this technique with great impact on two students: one, a 5-year-old boy with autism, Ryan (Buggey, 2005); the second, a 7-year-old boy with Down syndrome, Alan. Before we initiated VSM with these students, both used only one-word verbalizations and rarely initiated conversation.

Parents and teachers were recruited to prompt verbalizations from Ryan and Alan. Their words were then cut and pasted onto the work area of iMovie, and then selected and pasted into two-, three-, and four-word sentences. Key to sentence construction was getting Ryan and Alan to say verbs. They said "go," "play," "eat," and "throw." This allowed us to construct a variety of sentences such as "I go home" and "I go to school." The resulting movies had excellent audio quality. The videos, however, were somewhat jerky, as the students' positions (and sometimes the room and their clothes) changed with each word. Still, when the viewer's eyes were closed, the sentences sounded almost perfect. (Ryan was the first student ever with whom this type of editing was used. In several subsequent cases, we focused on having the child imitate the words in the same room and tried to get multiple-word utterances so we could avoid the jerky and changing visual images.)

Reports from home and school were immediately positive for the child with Down syndrome. Alan's mother got quite emotional when she first heard him using the advanced language on his video. Both Alan's mother and teacher reported increases in his initiations, responding, and sentence length. Although there were no scientific controls in this case, Alan's mother collected examples of his verbalizations and they did indicate significant improvement. He went from saying only single words to making up to four-word utterances.

Ryan showed similar gains to Alan, but not at first. His video emphasized responding behaviors; thus, video clips of his schoolmates and teacher asking questions were embedded prior to his responses. After watching this video, Ryan showed some improvement in responding to questions, but this did not generalize to verbal initiations, as hoped. We hypothesized that including clips of the peers asking questions might have distracted Ryan from the salient feature of the movie: his talking. We therefore created a second movie with the peers edited out so that Ryan was the sole star of the video. The results were much more positive following this revision, with Ryan showing accelerated gains in responding and good gains in initiations. Two days after first viewing the new video, Ryan met me at the door to the school with a "Hi, Dr. Tom."

To date, the article I published in 2005 in the *Journal of Positive Behavior Interventions* about using VSM with Ryan is the only one to describe this form of language intervention with children with developmental disabilities. This method is certainly worthy of more study.

Case Study 7—Edie's Interview
(Role Play with a High School Student; Using Two Cameras)

Edie was an 18-year-old with autism who was enrolled in a high school transition program that emphasized functional life and career skills. She was having particular problems learning the social skills that her family and professionals considered essential to gaining employment. In particular, her family feared that she could not conduct a good interview.

To help Edie learn interviewing skills, we set up a simulation of a job interview in the guidance office. This site resembled many office sites, with a waiting area and a receptionist/secretary. A local business woman agreed to serve as the interviewer. A team consisting of the business woman, Edie, and her teachers and parents sat down together to construct a storyboard representing the interview process and preparatory activities. The storyboard is presented on the next page.

We planned the storyboard to emphasize transitions in the interview process that required knowledge of social nuances such as greetings and farewells. We also included a scene related to Edie's difficulty waiting for long periods without fidgeting and standing and pacing. The storyboard ended up being a task-analysis of the interview process with special frames to highlight Edie's areas of weaknesses.

The filming process went very smoothly, except that Edie tended to read the script "robotically." We worked with her on intonation and speaking from memory. It took several takes before we had enough footage of natural-sounding conversation. Edie also tended to fidget while sitting in the waiting area, but this was easy to deal with in the editing process rather than by asking her to sit still in the simulation. We asked her parents to assist by taking footage at home of Edie picking out clothes and putting on make-up. This was a good way to invest her parents in the process and allowed us to get authentic footage of her preparation for the interview.

To film Edie's interview, we used two cameras. When she was alone in a scene, one camera focused on Edie and the other shot her from a different angle. During the greetings and interviews, we aimed cameras at each participant. The two-camera system allowed us to do more close-ups and to use the zoom lens to move back to more wide-angled shots. In the end, using two cameras did not make a great deal

Edie's Interview

Choose nice clothes to wear.	Be on time.
Wait quietly until you are called.	Greet everyone in the interview. Shake hands. Introduce yourself.
Answer questions politely, don't be in a hurry.	Thank everyone. Stand up to leave and shake hands again.

of difference between this video and one we would normally take, but being able to move from one angle to another during a dialog made the video more "polished." We called this the "60 Minutes" procedure because it resembled the effect often seen on TV interview shows.

Edie greatly enjoyed the filming of her movie. She was given time during the mornings before classes started to view herself and was also allowed to watch it one more time during the day at a time of her choosing. Edie is still in school, so we do not know the practical outcome of her video in terms of her career. However, in subsequent interview simulations, she performed exceedingly well and her parents and teachers reported an overall change in her general confidence level.

Case Study 8—Harley, Shopping at Target
(Combining Photo Visual Schedules with VSM)

Harley was a 7-year-old boy who had moderate to severe autism, as well as significant behavior problems. His parents were quite concerned about their inability to take Harley with them when they ran errands to local businesses. His behavior in stores was so negative that they had given up on allowing him to accompany them. This restricted the parents' ability to run errands and go shopping to times when one of them could stay home with Harley.

In order to do the storyboard for this project, a special education supervisor and Harley's teaching assistant accompanied Harley and his mother on a shopping trip to Target. The two special education professionals recorded the steps of the excursion and noted times when Harley behaved inapproriately. The sequenced steps—including walking across the street with Mom, entering the store, choosing a video and placing those not selected back in their proper location, and checking out—became the scenes on the storyboard. In addition, these steps were used to illustrate a visual schedule for Harley. This entailed taking still images from the video that best illustrated each step, laminating them, and attaching them to poster board with Velcro.

The visual schedule was used to prepare Harley for his next trip to Target so that he could review the steps involved and "surprises" would be minimized. The schedule was also used while at the store so he could keep track of where he was in the sequence and see what activity was coming up. His mother carried the schedule. When Harley finished a step in the visit, he took that image off the board. The aspects of the trip that proved most problematic for Harley were checking out, choosing a video, and following directions. Handling these situations effectively became important parts of his final VSM video.

Harley's next trip to Target was videotaped in its entirety. (It should be noted that permission to do this activity was obtained from the store manager, and the cashiers at the checkout were also briefed about was occurring. Walking into a store with cameras rolling might not be appreciated by everyone.) One of Harley's behaviors that drew a lot of attention at the store was making whining sounds that picked up in intensity when he was in a challenging situation. Harley made these sounds the whole time he was at the checkout counter. He did, however, hand the money to the cashier and take the bag with purchased videos.

The editing process was challenging mainly due to Harley's vocalizations. These could not be totally removed. There were also several audible prompts from Harley's mother about putting items back on the shelves. These adult prompts followed by Harley's compliance were important to keep in the video. By the time Harley checked out, his whining had turned to crying, so it was necessary to edit out the sounds. The special education supervisor accomplished this by overlaying a narration onto the checkout scene. This was very easy to do with iMovie plus a microphone hooked up to the computer. (Most newer computers have a mike built in.) Once she had made a voice recording stating "Here's Harley checking out and handing the money to the cashier," it was just a matter of clicking it and dragging it to the point on the video where Harley began to cry. The volume of this scene on the original video was turned off at the point where he approached the checkout counter (another simple click-and-drag procedure).

Two copies of the final edited video were made so that Harley could watch his video at school and at home. He watched them avidly in both locations. Reports from his parents indicated that he made such dramatic improvements in his disruptive and noncompliant behaviors that they now felt comfortable taking him on errands and shopping.

This case study was carried out by Wendy Ashcroft, a special education supervisor in the Memphis area, and remains the best example of a self-modeling video I have ever seen.

Case Study 9—Haley, Interacting with Her Friends
(Editing to Create the Illusion of Desired Behavior)

Haley was a 3-year-old diagnosed with pervasive developmental delay. She averted her eyes and turned her whole body away when adults or peers approached. Her oral vocabulary was only slightly delayed, yet she rarely used language to communicate with children and adults in her class. On the playground she would play by herself, often roaming around and making brief stops at equipment, especially the swings. In her classroom, a buddy system had been established, linking children with and without disabilities. During transitions, a classmate would be paired with her. Sometimes the peer would take Haley's hand, but she would pull away. The other children seemed to give up on Haley because they were not getting any reciprocal responses following their initiations.

We asked two of Haley's classmates to co-star in a movie we were making about Haley. Filming was carried out on the playground and in a small room in the school where we had gathered up some toys. The storyboard was done slightly differently than usual. Rather than illustrating the steps in an activity, we concentrated on discovering which activities Haley was most likely to participate in with other children present. We observed the peers on the playground and looked for simple examples of them interacting with each other. Haley's parents and teachers then sat down together and talked about which of these behaviors Haley would most likely do. We settled on the following interactions: a) pushing another child on the swing; b) playing near a classmate in the sandbox; c) swinging with other children on a tire swing; and d) holding hands with a peer when transitioning to and from the classroom. These became the scenes in our storyboard.

Capturing the swinging behaviors was easy because Haley enjoyed doing this. Even the tire swing was easy to film, although there was still some eye gaze aversion. The sandbox was also easy, as this was one of Haley's favorite activities, and the proximity of the other girls did not seem to bother Haley as long as she was engaged in her own play. Filming Haley holding hands with a peer involved a little patience, but after four trips back and forth, we had 30 seconds of footage.

The two co-stars were asked to try to engage Haley in play in the locations decided upon. At least, they were to play near Haley, occasionally ask her questions, hand her objects, and push her on the swing. We took all of this footage and combined it so that it appeared that interactions were occurring. For example, one of the girls offered Haley a shovel in the sandbox, which she ignored. She did use the shovel later, so we placed that footage immediately after the offer was made. We looked at the footage of her playing with the shovel and selected a section where Haley made a movement that best approximated taking it from the peer. There was a moment where she held the shovel out away from her and stared at it and that was where we started the clip following the peer's offer. We also interspersed clips throughout the video that showed Haley smiling and laughing.

Haley enjoyed watching the video each morning and asked to see it (usually by pointing to the small TV-VCR combo we provided for this purpose). Some changes in Haley's behavior were immediate, albeit subtle. She held hands with peers for much longer periods during transitions and started to move closer to other children on the playground. She still exhibited the avoidance behavior if children approached her in the sandbox area, but in the swing area, she seemed much more sociable and actually initiated requests for other children to push her. Haley's teachers and parents reported that these gains were significant. We are making a second video of Haley using clips we didn't use in the first video with the hope that we can build on these initial gains.

5 | Frequently Asked Questions

1. How do I know if my child has the prerequisite skills in self-recognition and attention to benefit from video self-modeling?

If your child plays in front of a mirror or responds to his image in the camcorder viewfinder (e.g., making faces, sticking out his tongue, or changing head positions), he probably has sufficient skills in self-recognition. Attention is more difficult to judge. But you will already know whether your child can sustain eye contact with a video screen for three

Video self-modeling seems to be effective starting with children over 2, although little is known about how young you can go.

minutes, and that can serve as a predictor of whether he can attend to a video of himself. To determine whether your child can attend to a self-modeling video, you may need to observe him watching the actual video.

2. Does it help to know the "function" of a behavior before you try to change it through VSM? What is the role of functional behavior assessment (FBA) in VSM?

Certainly it is important to know the function of the behavior when trying to decide on an appropriate replacement behavior that will become the focus of the video. If your child or student has a problematic behavior and the function of it is unknown, a functional behavior assessment is probably advisable, whether or not VSM is being considered as an intervention. VSM is one of a myriad of possible interventions that may arise out of an FBA. However, because VSM is relatively new, it may be up to you to introduce the idea to the IEP team.

The one great advantage that VSM presents relative to a positive behavior support plan is the fact that the method is inherently positive. FBAs require an analysis of the antecedents (events leading up to the behavior) of a behavior, the behavior itself, and the consequences. Knowledge of each of these factors can be of great value when designing your VSM video.

Tantrums provide a good example of how knowledge gained through an FBA can be applied. The antecedents may include environmental situations related to the tantrums as well as actions of people in the environment that serve to trigger the tantrum.

A self-modeling video that involves role playing a behavior will need to feature these antecedents. For example, if you know that Roger tends to have tantrums during free-play or recess when he is asked to stop playing and come inside for reading class, the first scene in the video should be shot in the recess area. The teacher might be shown prompting Roger to stop doing something. (I would not depict the tantrums you are trying to eliminate, however.)

Thus, you are filming both the natural environment and the triggers associated with the tantrum. But instead of filming the tantrum that usually occurs as a result of these antecedents, Roger will be instructed to act out an appropriate response. Roger can even be asked to verbalize a response to the teacher's verbal prompt (e.g., "I don't need to cry. I can come inside and pass out the reading books"). Finally, the consequences of the behavior will be altered on the self-modeling video as well. Perhaps ordinarily the consequence is that Roger is able to avoid reading class when he throws a tantrum. Instead, the video can depict him actively engaged in passing out reading books. Roger can be shown receiving praise from the adults and/or peers for his "mature" behavior. Cheering and clapping can also be added if you are using computer software to edit the movie.

3. Can VSM be used in conjunction with ABA programs?

Applied behavior analysis (ABA) is a mainstay of behavioral therapy for many children and has more supporting evidence of efficacy than any other method. VSM should not replace ABA in a treatment regimen. However, VSM can be used to supplement more conventional methods, including ABA.

ABA and other positive behavior supports are based on working towards a distinct goal that can usually be represented in visual imagery via VSM. Allowing the child to view the intended outcome (feedforward) has the potential to accelerate strides to the desired behavior. For example, if the goal for your child is to use a fork when eating, to respond to other children's greetings at school, or to complete a job application, you could make a self-modeling video to show him actually doing those things.

Likewise, VSM can be used in reading instruction to increase interest and to help elevate a child's self-confidence and efficacy. Limiting frustration may go a long way in helping the student control behavior. Normal or remedial reading instruction should continue as outlined in the IEP, however.

4. Can VSM be used in conjunction with other strategies commonly used to teach skills to people with developmental disabilities?

Video self-modeling is one method among many that can be brought to bear on an instructional or behavioral issue. In some cases, it can be a logical extension of existing strategies. For example, if attempts at adult- and peer-modeling have failed, moving on to self-modeling might be the next step considered. Or, if you are having limited success with Social Stories or Comic Strip Conversations as developed by Carol Gray (very similar to role playing and storyboarding discussed in the book), VSM will allow you to animate those strategies and to place the child at the center of the method.

5. Is there anything you can or should do if your child or student won't watch the video, even though he usually likes watching videos?

Having the child attend to the video is essential. On the other hand, putting pressure on the child to watch the video could result in him or her putting up defenses and resisting even more adamantly. It is important to allow children to watch their video on their terms. There should be no problem in offering some form of incentive or reward for viewing; however, that probably won't affect how much attention the child pays to the screen. If he is not interested in the video, then it won't be successful.

6. Is it OK to leave the video out at home and let the child watch it whenever he pleases?

That is actually the preferred method. The more the child can take the lead and the more interest he or she exhibits in the video, the better.

7. How should you respond if your child or student says something negative about the video or himself (e.g., "I look dumb")?

There are a few ways to handle this during the filming and editing. During editing we always select the most attractive or flattering frame to use as the background for the first scene. This always includes written titles, verbally labeling the behavior, and cheering/clapping. (The cheering crowd sounds like something you would hear at the beginning of a rock concert. I think teens and young adults, as well as younger children, would benefit from that type of reinforcement.) Beginning the video in this way usually helps the person view it in a positive light, especially if you are able to play up the "movie star" aspect of the video.

It is also helpful to let the "star" choose the clothes he wants to wear during filming, or to otherwise give him a chance to make himself look good. Choosing "wardrobe" is similar to having the child help with the storyboard; it fosters "investment" in the project. Also the addition of "make-up" and "wardrobe" will contribute to the idea of this being a real movie production.

It helps to know how the child feels about pictures of himself in general. A colleague of mine in school psychology had one situation with a young boy who had a partially repaired cleft palate. We were working on his responses to people who asked him to repeat himself due to his unclear speech. He was very sensitive to his appearance and frontal shots, so we filmed him entirely in profile.

If the child is so sensitive about his appearance that there is no way of working around it, then VSM may not be appropriate. If the experience is negative for the child, the method loses it effectiveness.

8. If you are using VSM at home and the video involves brothers or sisters, should they be allowed as much access to the video as the child with autism (for example, if the child with autism thinks it is his video alone)?

The easiest solution is to make two copies—one for each sibling—and personalize each. This is easy to do with video on a computer. If you use the camcorder-to-VCR or DVD method, you may have to do some additional editing. Do set rules for the sibling, however. Emphasize that VSM is a positive method and that she should not make any negative comments about the video's content or about her brother or sister's behavior depicted on the video.

9. Would it ever be a good idea to dub in speech for the child using another child's voice?

Maybe, depending on the child's own abilities and the nature of the specific behavior targeted. Of course, if he can't use speech, do not even target this as a behavior.

In one of our recent studies we actually used a peer's voice dubbed over the video of a child with autism. We wanted to increase his social interactions with peers on the playground. The boy was verbal, so we taped him saying things like "c'mon," "let's play," "chase me," etc. The problem was that his articulation made it hard for viewers (and perhaps himself) to understand what he was saying. To avoid this problem, we recorded a peer saying the same words and overlaid these words on the child's video.

I was afraid we would end up with something like a foreign language movie translated to English where the mouth and spoken words are not in sync (the Godzilla effect), but my graduate assistants were able to put the words in the iMovie work area and move the voice track right and left until there was an almost perfect fit. I hesitated to give my graduate students permission to do this because I felt uneasy about "tricking" the child with a voice that wasn't his.

Two factors made me decide to give this a try. One was that we do not hear what others hear when we speak. Many of us still think "is that me?" when we hear ourselves on recordings. Thus, there was a good chance that the child would recognize the peer's voice as his own. The second factor was that he could already say the words, so we were not going too far a field from his present abilities—articulation was the issue. In the end, the video worked very well and the child ended up making significantly more social initiations on the playground.

10. What about using a "hand model" for your child? For example, if you want him to learn to tie his shoes (or another motor skill), could you zoom in on another child's hands tying shoes, but show your child's face? Or is it just better to prompt the child himself through every step?

We have used face, hand, and leg models in our videos. We always depict our target child first and then switch to the model. For example, for young children with eating or feeding problems, we show the food, the child holding the fork or spoon, and that utensil going into our "face model's" mouth.

In one instance when we used "leg models" to increase children's social interactions with peers on the playground, the videos actually led to the children learning to use the slide. We originally wanted the children with autism to use a slide as part of their social interaction videos. There are double slides on the Siskin Children's Institute's playground and we thought it would be nice to have children holding hands as they went down the slide. It was easy to get one of the children to the top of the slides that had a broad standing area, but he would not take the plunge down the slide. So, we took footage of the child and a peer holding hands at the top of the slide and later we arranged to take video of peers from the waist down coming down the slide. Sliding was not our target behavior for this child. We just wanted him to interact more. A few days after he watched his video, he not only went down the slide unprompted, he got on a swing for the first time. Watching the video seemed to help him generalize to other playground skills not present on the video.

11. Is it OK to use VSM with a child who tends to persever-ate on movies? Is there any reason not to let him watch his movie 100 times in a row?

I suppose this depends on how effective the video is and how much the perseverative behavior affects the child's daily functioning. We had one four-year-old boy who began standing in front of reflective windows facing the preschool playground after watching his video about playing with friends. This became a ritual behavior, but his rate of interaction with peers also increased and it wasn't difficult to redirect him from the window.

One other thing to remember in a situation like this is that if changes don't occur soon after the child starts watching the video, they are unlikely to occur at all. So, if you don't see positive changes soon after completing the video, I think you could look more critically at the perseverative behavior.

One last point—I have never seen a child go overboard in watching his self-modeling video even when he was super-enthused about watching himself.

12. If a particular event is a known trigger for a prob-lem behavior, is it possible that making a video of that event and then showing it to the person could trigger that behavior? For example, if the sound of the fire alarm at school usually causes the child to have a meltdown, would watching a tape that includes that sound also cause a meltdown? Is there any way around this?

So far, I have not made a self-modeling video focusing on a trig-ger that is truly frightening to the child. Several times in this book, however, I referred to a study we did with two boys who had tantrums just about every day. We identified the triggers and then used each of these situations as a scene in the movie. We acted out line jumping, getting problems on homework assignments wrong, etc. We walked the children through these triggers by prompting them with lines to say and we emphasized what we were doing and often reminded them that we were acting. The types of triggers we dealt with here did not have the startle effect of a loud noise like a fire alarm.

It probably would be better to begin by trying to desensitize the child to the alarm. One way this might be done is to allow the child to go to the school on the weekends, and with subsequent ringings of the alarm, have him move closer and closer to the source. I imagine using a fire alarm in this way might cause problems with the local fire department, so either come to some arrangement with them first or use another source for the loud sound.

There also may be a way to work on desensitization using videos and video editing software. Both iMovie and Movie Maker allow easy control of volume. It would be simple to lower the volume on the video just as the alarm goes off and bring it up when the alarm has stopped. It would be possible to slowly bring up the sound intensity across subsequent movie viewings. I think this method would be worth a try and might save the firemen some anxiety.

13. If you are taking hours of videotape across several days, trying to get footage of the child doing something he rarely does, is it important that actors wear the same clothes in every take?

This would be helpful for the continuity of the video, but I have found that inconsistencies like clothes and position changes do not adversely affect results.

14. Is VSM technically "assistive technology?" If so, are you aware of any ways to get school districts to pay for cameras, needed software, etc.? ("Assistive Technology Device" is defined in the IDEA Improvement Act of 2004 as "any item, piece of equipment, or product system, whether acquired commercially off the shelf, modified, or customized, that is used to increase, maintain, or improve functional capabilities of a child with a disability.") At some point, do you think parents may be able to get help with VSM from Assistive Technology Centers?

I'd have to put on my lawyer hat to answer this one and that hat doesn't fit me very well. I imagine schools and insurance companies would be reluctant to see VSM categorized as assistive technology. That said, I doubt whether this has been tested yet. It might be worth a try to get VSM into an Individualized Education Program (IEP) as assistive technology. But, when you think about the equipment needed, what school does not own a camcorder and several computers? That is all you really need.

As far as the Assistive Technology Centers go, I would hope they explore VSM as a treatment option. They, more than any other group, should have fewer problems with, and less fear of, the needed technology. Again, the investment for equipment needed may be zero, while the possible applications with children with cognitive, physical, or sensory challenges are endless.

When I think about the most efficient way to bring VSM into use in schools and clinical settings, I think of therapists and support personnel taking the lead. Occupational and physical therapists, speech-language pathologists, and guidance counselors should all experiment with VSM. I think that once people have gained a little experience using VSM, they will quickly realize the potential benefits and the range of possible applications for this very positive method.

References

Bandura, A. (1969). *Principles of Behavior Modification*. New York: Holt, Rinehart & Winston.

Bandura, A. (1997). *Self-efficacy: The Exercise of Control*. New York: Freeman.

Bellini, S. & Akullian, J. (2007). A meta-analysis of video modeling and video self-modeling interventions for children and adolescents with autism spectrum disorders. *Exceptional Children, 73*, 261-84.

Bellini, S., Akullian, J., & Hopf, A. (2007). Increasing social engagement in young children with autism spectrum disorders using video self-modeling. *School Psychology Review, 36,* 80-90.

Bray, M. A. & Kehle, T. J. (1996). Self-modeling as an intervention for stuttering. *School Psychology Review, 25 (3)*, 358-69.

Buggey, T. (1995). An examination of the effectiveness of videotaped self-modeling in teaching specific linguistic structures to preschoolers. *Topics in Early Childhood Special Education, 15*, 434-58.

Buggey, T. (1996). *Efficacy of videotaped self-modeling with preschoolers with language delay*. Memphis: TN: The University of Memphis. (ERIC Document Reproduction service No. ED 390 211).

Buggey, T., Toombs, K., Gardener, P., & Cervetti, M. (1998). Self-modeling as a technique to train response behaviors in children with autism. *Journal of Positive Behavior Intervention, 1,* 205-14.

Buggey, T. (2005). Applications of video self-modeling with children with autism in a small private school. *Focus on Autism and Other Developmental Disabilities,* 20, 180-204.

Buggey, T. (2007). A picture is worth. . . : Video self-modeling applications at school and home. *Journal of Positive Behavior Interventions, 9 (2),* 151-158.

Christakis, D. A., Zimmerman, F. J., DiGiuseppe, D. L., & McCarty, C. A. (2004). Early television exposure and subsequent attentional problems in children. *Pediatrics, 113(4),* 708-13.

Creer, T. L. & Miklich, D. R. (1970). The application of a self-modeling procedure to modify inappropriate behavior: A preliminary report. *Behavior Research and Therapy, 8,* 91-92.

Davis, M. W. (2004). The effects of an augmented self-modeling intervention on the on-task and off-task classroom behaviors of students with developmental disabilities. Master's Thesis. University of Central Arkansas, Dept. of Psychology and Counseling.

Decker, M. (2001). The effects of video-taped self-modeling on reading fluency in elementary-aged students with reading delays. Doctoral Dissertation, The University of Memphis.

Delano, M. (2007). Improving written language performance of adolescents with Asperger syndrome. *Journal of Applied Behavior Analysis, 40(2),* 342-51.

Dowrick, P. W. (1977). Video replay as observational learning from oneself. *Unpublished paper, University of Auckland School of Medicine, Department of Psychiatry and Behavioral Science.*

Dowrick, P. W. (1983). Self-modeling. In P. W. Dowrick & J. Biggs (Eds.), *Using Video: Psychological and Social Applications* (pp. 105-24). New York: Wiley.

Dowrick, P. W., & Dove, C. (1980). The use of self-modeling to improve the swimming performance of spina bifida children. *Journal of Applied Behavior Analysis, 13*, 51-56.

Dowrick, P. W., & Hood, M. (1981). Comparison of self-modeling and small cash incentives in a sheltered workshop. *Journal of Applied Psychology, 66*, 394-97.

Dowrick, P. W., Kim-Rupnow, W. S., & Power, T. J. (2006). Video feedforward for reading. *The Journal of Special Education, 39 (4)*, 194-207.

Dowrick, P. W. & Raeburn, J. (1977). Video editing and medication to produce a therapeutic self-model. *Journal of Consulting and Clinical Psychology, 45*, 1156-58.

Dowrick, P. W. & Ward, K. M. (1997). Video feedforward in the support of a man with intellectual disability and inappropriate sexual behaviour. *Journal of Intellectual and Developmental Disability, 22 (3)*, 147-60.

Duncan, G., Dowsette, G., Claessens, C., Magnunson, A., Huston, K., Klebanov, A., Pagani, K., Feinstein, L., Engel, L., Brooks-Gunn, M., Sexton, J., Duckworth, H. & Japel, K. (2007). School readiness and later achievement. *Developmental Psychology, 43 (6)*, 1428-46.

Grandin, T. (1996). *Thinking in Pictures.* New York: Vintage Press.

Gray, S. & Shelley, M. (2007). *StoryMovies.* Columbia, SC: Accelerations Educational Software.

Greenberg, D., Buggey, T. & Bond C. (2003). Effects of video self-modeling on reading skills and attitudes of at-risk readers. (ERIC Document Reproduction Service).

Haarmann, B. S., & Greelis, M. T. (1982). Video therapy case study: The therapeutic use of edited videotapes as a primary means of behavioral intervention in the shaping of appropriate grammatical and contextual use of language. *Journal of Special Education Technology, 5*, 52-56.

Hartley, E. T., Bray, M. A., & Kehle, T. J. (1998). Self-Modeling as an intervention to increase classroom participation. *Psychology in the Schools, 35(4)*, 363-72.

Hepting, N. & Goldstein, H. (1996). Requesting by preschoolers with developmental disabilities: Videotaped self-modeling and learning of new linguistic structures. *Topics in Early Childhood Special Education, 16(3)*, 407-27.

Hitchcock, C. H., Dowrick, P. W., & Prater, M. A. (2003). Video self-modeling intervention in school-based settings: A review. *Remedial and Special Education, 24 (1)*, 36-46.

Hitchcock, C. H., Prater, M. A., & Dowrick, P. W. (2004). Reading comprehension and fluency: Examining the effects of tutoring and video self-modeling on first-grade students with reading difficulties. *Learning Disability Quarterly, 27 (2)*, 89-103.

Hosford, R. E. (1981). Self-as-a-model: A cognitive social learning technique. *The Counseling Psychologist, 9,* 45-61.

Hosford, R. E., & Brown, S. D. (1976). Using social modeling procedures to improve undergraduate instruction (Tech. Rep. Contract No. 8-407674-07427). Santa Barbara: University of California Innovative Teaching Project.

Kahn, J. S., Kehle, T. J., Jenson, W. R., & Clark, E. (1990). Comparison of cognitive-behavioral, relaxation, and self-modeling interventions for depression among middle-school students. *School Psychology Review, 19,* 196-211.

Kehle, T. J., Bray, M. A., Margiano, S. G., Theodore, L. A., & Zhou, Z. (2002). Self-modeling as an effective intervention for students with serious emotional disturbance: Are we modifying children's memories? *Psychology in the Schools, 39 (2)*, 203-207.

Kehle, T. J. & Gonzales, F. P. (1991). Self-modeling for emotional and social concerns of childhood. In P. W. Dowrick (Ed.), *A Practical Guide to Video in the Behavioral Sciences*. New York: John Wiley & Sons.

Kehle, T. J., Madaus, M. R., Baratta, V. S., Bray, M. A. (1998). Augmented self-modeling as a treatment for children with selective mutism. *Journal of School Psychology, 36 (3),* 247-60.

Kimball, J. W., Kinney, E. M., Taylor, B. A., & Stromer, R. (2003). Lights, camera, action! Using engaging computer-cued activity schedules. *Teaching Exceptional Children, 36,* 40-45.

Kimball, J. W., Kinney, E. M., Taylor, B. A., & Stromer, R. (2004). Video enhanced activity schedules for children with autism: A promising package for teaching social skills. *Education and Treatment of Children, 27,* 280-98.

Lewis, M., & Brooks-Gunn, J. (1979). The search for the origins of self: Implications for social behavior and intervention. In L. Montada (Ed.), *Brennpunkte der entwicklungspsychologie (pp. 157-72).* Stuttgart, Germany: W. Kohlhammer.

Lovaas, O. I. (1987). Behavioral treatment and normal educational and intellectual functioning in young autistic children. *Journal of Consulting and Clinical Psychology, 55*(1), 3-9.

McCurdy, B. L. & Shapiro, E. S. (1988). Self-observation and the reduction of inappropriate classroom behavior. *Journal of School Psychology, 26,* 371-78.

Meharg, S. S. & Lipsker, L. E. (1991). Parent training using videotape self-modeling. *Child & Family Behavior Therapy, 13,* 1-26.

Miklich, D. R., Chida, T. L., & Danker-Brown, P. (1977). Behavior modification by self-modeling without subject awareness. *Journal of Behavior and Experimental Psychiatry, 8,* 125-30.

Neumann, L. (2004). *Video Modeling: A Visual Teaching Method for Children with Autism,* 2nd ed. Brandon, FL: Willerik Publishing (www.ideasaboutautism.com).

Pigott, H. E., & Gonzales, F. P. (1987). Efficacy of self-modeling in treating an electively mute child. *Journal of Clinical Child Psychology, 16,* 106-10.

Schunk, D. H. & Hanson, A. R. (1989). Self-modeling and children's cognitive skill learning. *Journal of Educational Psychology, 81,* 155-63.

Siegler, R. S. (1991). *Children's Thinking* (2nd ed.). Englewood Cliffs, NJ: Prentice Hall.

Wert, B. W., & Neisworth, J. T. (2003). Effects of video self-modeling on spontaneous requesting in children with autism. *Journal of Positive Behavior Interventions, 5,* 300-305.

Woltersdorf, M. A. (1992). Videotape self-modeling in the treatment of attention-deficit hyperactivity disorder. *Child & Family Behavior Therapy, 14,* 53-73.

Wright, C. & Smith, D. (2009). The effect of PETTLEP imagery on strength performance. *International Journal of Sport and Exercise Psychology.*

Glossary

Baseline: The rate, frequency, or duration of behaviors prior to intervention; the person's present functioning level.

Dependent variables: In research studies, this is what you want to change; the target behavior. *See* Independent variables.

Feedforward: An aspect of self-modeling in which children can view themselves as they might be performing or behaving at a future time.

FireWire: A cable for high speed data transfer between a computer and an auxiliary device such as a camcorder. Also known as an IEEE-1394.

Generalization: Using behavior that was originally learned in one setting or with certain people in different settings and/or with different people.

Graphic organizers: Diagrams or illustrations that help students organize information.

IEP (Individualized Education Program): A document that details the special education program to be provided to a child with disabilities aged three and up. The document specifies individualized goals for the student, services to be provided to enable the student to meet the goals, the setting where the services will be provided, etc.

IFSP (Individualized Family Service Plan): A document that specifies the early intervention services to be provided to an infant or toddler with disabilities (aged birth to 2) and his or her family.

Independent variables: In research studies, this is the intervention; what you are using to affect dependent variables.

Informed consent: Agreement by parents to allow their children to participate in an activity or procedure that is based on their complete understanding of what is entailed.

Interval recording: A method of data collection where observation periods are divided into smaller, equal time periods (e.g., 10-minute intervals).

Learning curve: A sine-shaped line that illustrates the rate at which new skills are learned.

Maintenance: The capacity of behaviors to be sustained when treatment or intervention is withdrawn.

Mand: An independent request for an object (e.g., cookies) or a condition (e.g., silence).

Multiple-baseline: An extension of single-subject research design in which several individuals or behaviors are charted. The researchers begin collecting baseline data on all of the behaviors and/or individuals at the same time, but start intervention at different times with each.

Perseveration: 1. Extraordinary and lasting obsession with details or occurrences that others consider minor. 2. Engaging in movements such as rocking or hand flapping that are often repetitive and unrelated to a known stimulus.

Positive self-review: A form of self-modeling aimed at honing skills already learned; accomplished by watching one's own best performances.

Self-efficacy: The confidence felt by people regarding their ability to successfully carry out a task.

Self-monitoring: A method aimed at making someone more aware of his or her behavior and subsequently taking control of that behavior. Children are typically asked to do behavior "checks" on themselves over a time interval following a prompt (such as a reminder from the teacher or an egg timer). The act of observation alone often has a positive effect. Children record their behavior when prompted and thus get a visual image of how often they engage in that behavior. Eventually the prompts and self-checks are faded as the children become more aware of their own behavior and develop self-control.

Self-observation: Viewing unedited videos of one's own behavior or performance that contain both positive and negative elements.

Single-subject: A research design with baseline, intervention, and sometimes withdrawal phases that is used to track changes in an individual.

Spiral curriculum: A method of teaching in which concepts and skills are taught sequentially and incrementally spaced out over time. Review of content previously taught is also included.

Storyboard: 1. A graphic representation of the scenes and sequence of a movie. 2. An area in video editing software where you store and edit the video clips you want to keep.

Task analysis: Breaking down situations, tasks, or complex behavior into their component parts or steps.

Time-sampling: A data collection technique in which an observer records data periodically over identical lengths of time (e.g., the first 5 minutes of every hour).

Visual schedule: A visual representation of planned activities using symbols (words, pictures, picture symbols, or photographs) that are presented in the order in which the activities occur.

Index

Italic page numbers indicate tables or figures

About the Author

Tom Buggey, Ph.D., received his master's degree in special education from Clarion University of Pennsylvania and his doctoral degree in early intervention from Penn State University. He conducts research at the Siskin Center for Child and Family Research at The Siskin Children's Institute in Chattanooga and is a professor and the Siskin Chair of Excellence in Early Childhood Special Education at the University of Tennessee at Chattanooga. He and his wife, Ann, live in Hixson, Tennessee.